The Genius of the Roman Rite

The Genius of the Roman Rite

On the Reception and Implementation of the New *Missal*

Keith F. Pecklers, S.J.

A PUEBLO BOOK

Liturgical Press   Collegeville, Minnesota
www.litpress.org

Published in the United States and Canada by Liturgical Press,
Collegeville, Minnesota 56321

www.litpress.org

First published 2009

ISBN 978–0-8146–6021-8

Cover design by David Manahan, O.S.B.
Cover illustration by Frank Kacmarcik, Obl.S.B.
Typeset by Free Range Book Design *&* Production Ltd
Printed and bound in Great Britain by the MPG Books Group

For Francis Campbell, British Ambassador to the Holy See.
Committed Catholic, Trusted Diplomat,
and Loyal Friend

Table of Contents

Introduction

The Roman Rite has evolved over the centuries in very diverse contexts and situations, and it has endured to our own day precisely because of its capacity to adapt and be shaped by the distinct cultures where it has been celebrated. Indeed, today when we speak of 'the Roman Rite' we would need to ask ourselves 'which one?,' since the pure and classical Roman Rite only existed from the fifth through the eighth centuries before it came into contact with other rites of the Church. In 2002, the Latin third edition of the *Missale Romanum* was promulgated and in subsequent years episcopal conferences around the world have been hard at work in producing vernacular translations of that Latin text.

As the English-speaking world plans to receive and implement the English translation of that *Missal* in the next few years, this book is offered as an instrument of catechesis in helping clergy and laity alike to better grasp the rationale for the new translations by considering the wider context of the Roman Rite itself. Chapter 1 offers a brief historical sweep of the Roman liturgy – how it was influenced by the Roman cultural genius and shaped by Roman court ceremonial, tracing its history through the sixteenth-century reforms of the Council of Trent (1545–63). Chapter 2 treats the liturgical reforms of the Second Vatican Council (1962–65) and evaluates how those reforms have been implemented and lived out since those heady days of the Council. Chapter 3 provides some needed background of how the translation process has been constituted since Vatican II: the rationale and principles for liturgical translations, the role played by various episcopal conferences and the process employed by the International Commission on English in the Liturgy (ICEL) charged with the task of translating the Latin liturgical texts into English. Chapter 4 examines the 2002 *General Instruction on the*

Roman Missal through the historical lens of its antecedents prior to the Council of Trent. This text serves as a sort of Preface to the *Roman Missal* and offers the liturgical choreography for a proper and unified celebration of the Roman Rite. The final chapter will explore what's inside the new *Missal* itself – the changes which will need to be implemented, and some of the concrete challenges which the ICEL translators faced in their work.

This book is based on a number of lectures I have given on related topics, and the work is much improved as a result of discussions with those who hosted me at the various institutions and their feedback on what I presented. Chapter 1 was originally a lecture given at the Orthodox Theological Faculty in Belgrade, Serbia, and again at the Presbyterian Seminary and Theological College in Seoul, South Korea. The base for the second chapter was a lecture given at the Catholic University of America, Washington, D.C. The final three chapters are the result of a series of talks I gave to the bishops and priests of the Archdiocese of Brisbane, Australia, on the implementation of the new *Missal*.

I wish to acknowledge my gratitude to a number of individuals. Gregory Collins, O.S.B., of Glenstal Abbey, Limerick, Ireland, first suggested the title 'The Ethos of the Roman Rite' when I was concerned that entitling my Belgrade lecture 'The Genius of the Roman Rite' after Edmund Bishop's classic essay might sound too self-congratulatory to the Serbian Orthodox. My thanks to Dennis Smolarski, S.J. of Santa Clara University, Santa Clara, California, for providing me with very helpful material on the *General Instruction on the Roman Missal*. I am grateful to Reverend Paul Turner, Pastor of Saint Munchin Parish in Cameron, Missouri, for his wise advice on how best to approach the Brisbane lectures and for recommending a helpful strategy regarding implementation of the *Missal*. Heartfelt thanks to Reverend Peter Williams, Executive Secretary of the Australian Bishops' Commission for Liturgy, for providing historical information on the Leeds Group. To Reverend Mark R. Francis, C.S.V., Superior General of the Clerics of Saint Viator, friend and colleague, my gratitude for carefully reading the manuscript and making helpful recommendations on the text. Much of this work was written at the Hekima Jesuit School of Theology, Nairobi, Kenya, and I'm very grateful to the Hekima Jesuit community for the warm welcome I received there and for the companionship. My thanks to Robin Baird Smith of Continuum, London, for his interest in publishing this work and for his ongoing support. Finally, my deepest gratitude to my mother and brother for all their love and support.

Keith F. Pecklers, S.J.

The Evolution of the Roman Rite

1

Introduction

On 8 May 1899, the British Historian Edmund Bishop gave a conference for the Historical Research Society at Westminster in London, entitled 'The Genius of the Roman Rite.' That paper, later published in 1918 in his classic volume *Liturgica Storica: Papers on the Liturgy and Religious Life of the Western Church* has forever changed the way historians of the Roman liturgy understand and describe its unique characteristics – its 'ethos.' Bishop concluded his Westminster lecture with these words: 'If I had to indicate in two or three words only the main characteristics which go to make up the genius of the Roman Rite, I should say that those characteristics were essentially soberness and sense.'[1]

From the inspiration of Bishop's groundbreaking essay, this first chapter will endeavor to get at the heart of the Roman Rite – what Bishop called 'the native spirit animating and penetrating that rite which differentiates it from others.'[2] We will do this through an exploration of how the Roman Rite evolved in its cultural ethos; its eventual contact with other rites, thereby creating a 'hybrid' Roman Rite; and a consideration of the liturgical reforms of the Sixteenth Century Council of Trent which lasted until the twentieth century's Second Vatican Council.

The Roman Cultural/Religious Context in the Second and Third Centuries

To arrive at the origins of the classic Roman Rite from the fifth to the eighth centuries, we must begin even earlier in the cultural and religious context of ancient Rome. Roman religion in the first century of the Christian era was an extraordinary mix of cults existing side by side, many of which included various superstitions. There were, of course, also outside influences coming into Rome from elsewhere. Christian Rome had so many immigrants and visitors, some of whom, like Montanus of Phyrigia and his late second century apocalyptic movement, led to erroneous notions. In general, these early Mediterranean religions were fascinated with signs and omens, ghosts, divination, and astrology. Cicero referred to the Roman rites of initiation as 'those mysteries by which we are trained out of undiscipline to human ways.'

'Those mysteries' included sacramental or symbolic actions: sacred meals; weddings; fertility and birth rites; baptisms; investitures with sacred garments; rites of death and resurrection in the form of symbolic journeys. Roman rites and mysteries were presided over by priests and mystagogues whose teaching was referred to as 'mystagogy.' Thus, one finds a great variety of religious cults responding to the vast amount of people in the Roman Empire. As long as the tranquility of the state was not disturbed, those new religions were allowed to continue and grow. Christianity was no exception in this early period – especially because at least some saw it as an outgrowth of Judaism which was already diffused throughout the empire with synagogues in every town.

Tolerance toward Christianity was short-lived, however. Christians came to be regarded as suspicious and their secrecy and discretion (meeting in homes, etc.) led to strange ideas and accusations against them. It was precisely for this reason that Justin Martyr wrote his *Apology* to the Roman Emperor around the year 150, attempting to convince the Emperor that what Roman Christians did when they gathered for the Sunday Eucharist was to celebrate a ritual meal that did not involve cannibalistic practices of drinking human blood or eating human flesh as had been rumored.

What we can observe in this early period is a significant amount of contact between Roman Christianity and the presence of mystery cults such as Mithra – the Persian God of light and wisdom.[3] Mithraism gradually spread through the Roman

Empire in the first century and reached its peak in the third, until it gradually faded in the fourth century with the legalization of Christianity. Unlike other early Mediterranean religions, Mithraism shared a special relationship with Christianity: both religions evolved at the same time and grew within the same geographical regions, embodying two distinct responses to the same cultural challenges and issues.[4] In some cases, Christian apologists like Justin and Tertullian criticized or even mocked the ritual practices of their non-Christian contemporaries: Justin, for example, accused the worshipers of Mithras of counterfeiting the Christian Eucharist in its initiatory meal of bread and water.[5] Tertullian, for his part, mocked the initiation baths of Isis and Mithra, which despite their expense and elegance accomplished nothing, he argued, unlike Christian Baptism which brought purification and salvation with few words and at no expense.[6] There were also some very distinct differences. The Cult of Mithra, for example, initiated its followers in a bath of warm bull's blood rather than water.

But even despite such distinctions and the Apologists' criticisms of the ritual practices operative within these early Mediterranean religions, Christian rituals gradually incorporated cultural elements into them reinterpreting them for Christian usage. Rites of anointing entered the Roman Baptismal Liturgy as the practice had long been established within the Greco-Roman culture. Footwashing of the newly baptized along with the kissing of the feet was another practice that came from non-Christian traditions of the day but was gradually incorporated into the Rites of Christian Initiation. Acts of renunciation and acclamation were also graphically portrayed in the Baptismal ritual and clearly related to similar symbolic gestures in ancient Roman religions: turning to the West – the region of darkness – to renounce Satan; turning to the East – the region of light – to acclaim Christ. Worshiping *ad orientem* – toward the East – was also a common practice in the Cult of Mithra as they prayed toward the rising sun.

There are many other examples of the influence of mystery rites on Christian worship in Rome in this early period – especially within the Sacrament of Baptism. As noted by Justin

Martyr in the mid second century, Baptism was called 'Enlightenment.' But that same term was used simultaneously in the mystery cults of Isis and Mithra. Indeed, as we study the initiation process within Roman Christianity and the mystery religions, we find a common vocabulary: washing; initiation; illumination. We also find a similarity in the components of those initiation rites: the scrutinies; learning of sacred formulas; fasting; stripping naked for immersion in the font; the water bath by immersion; the putting on of the white garment; the meal of initiation; the post-baptismal period of mystagogy.

Similarly, there was a borrowing from or adapting to secular culture. A mixture of milk and honey that came to be given to the newly baptized was borrowed from the custom in ancient Rome when the *paterfamilias* welcomed the newborn into the family but also as a superstitious protection against evil spirits. In Roman noble households, the newborn was placed before the head of the family. If the child was deformed – or sometimes even just a girl when the parents wanted a boy – that newborn could be rejected and given to the servants to raise. But when the baby was accepted, the mixture of milk and honey was offered.

Tertullian mentions this practice in the Rite of Christian Initiation in North Africa, using the Latin term *susceptio* or *munus susceptionis* – a juridical term which signified, among other things, the father's legal acceptance or recognition of the newborn infant presented to him as his own. After Baptism, in the mind of Tertullian, the newborn was accepted (*susceptus*) by the Church as one of her own. The mixed drink was offered as a sign of welcome and recognition. Several centuries later, the *Apostolic Tradition* would also refer to this mixture of milk and honey offered to the neophyte. Tertullian borrowed military terms such as *sacramenti testatio* and *signaculum fidei* or promise of loyalty to the Roman Emperor, when he spoke of the Baptismal profession of faith. As always, those cultural elements were given a new Christological interpretation as they were introduced into Roman Christian worship, and Roman bishops used their mystagogical catecheses after they had baptized at Easter to explain the new symbolism.

The Legalization of Christianity and the Evolution of Roman Worship in the Fourth Century

With Constantine's victory over Maxentius at the Battle of the Milvian Bridge in the year 312 and the Edict of Milan of the following year (313), Christianity became a public religion, yet Constantine was limited in the ways he could serve the Roman Church. In fact, the Roman Forum remained pagan territory even after the Peace of Constantine. Along the *Via Sacra* within the Forum a series of pagan statues were erected between the years 337 and 341, among which can be found some old deities. Similar developments were found just outside Rome at the port town of Ostia Antica. Paganism was only definitively suppressed in Rome with the Christian Emperor Teodosius in the year 395. Then, the last members of the great Roman families who had not yet become Christian were forced to do so, even if they remained crypto-pagans.

While Constantine could not abolish the pagan cults, he gave greater privileges to the Christian bishops. For example, in the year 318, he conferred on bishops civil jurisdiction over court litigations which involved Christians. Thus the clergy acquired titles and insignia that state dignitaries enjoyed. While he could not destroy the pagan buildings, he could build impressive ones for the Christian cult like the Basilica of Saint John Lateran and its famous Baptistery. Some of those great buildings were privately financed while others were erected at public expense. Not surprisingly, places of Christian worship multiplied in this period and the liturgy at Rome gradually came into its own.

Liturgical language itself was influenced by the Church's integration into the socio-political structure of the Roman Empire. This is seen very clearly in the Veronese *libelli* of 558. Words like *ordo, gradus, dignitas, honor* were all used in the ordination rites of bishops, priests, and deacons, but they came from the hierarchy – the ranking system – of Roman government officials. Parallel to this Roman system, the clerical hierarchy was defined according to the rank and the corresponding dignity of office and honor. Thus, at this early period, Church offices were regarded, in some way, as equivalents of the Roman institution.

This is especially evident in the Roman Canon, the oldest extant *anaphora* of the Roman Church. The language is very juridical with solemn addresses and a clear rhetorical style. Other liturgical elements were borrowed from Roman practice. Kissing the altar and sacred images originated from gestures of reverence common within the Roman Empire. Prostrations, processions, and the use of incense and candles were all adapted from the ceremonials of the Roman Imperial Court. Likewise, the vesting of Roman clergy exhibits the same cultural borrowing as distinguishing clothing of Roman state officials was borrowed and reinterpreted.

The Peace of Constantine offered greater freedom for the development of the Roman liturgical calendar, as well. Christians in Rome began celebrating the birth of Christ around the year 336 on 25 December. Here again, there are cultural factors regarding the choice of date. Already in the year 274, followers of the Cult of Mithra kept the feast of the *Natale solis invicti* around the winter solstice. On 21 December, the shortest and darkest day of the year, Roman followers of Mithra celebrated the birth of the invincible sun. While there are several possible interpretations of why the Roman Church would have chosen 25 December for the festival of Christ's birth, it is certainly plausible that in establishing its own liturgical calendar there was also an inherent desire to counteract the pagan feasts.

A similar example can be found in the Roman feast of 22 February. During eight days in February, Romans celebrated the pagan festival of *Parentalia* in honor of their ancestors. Part of the celebration involved a funeral meal called *charistia* or *cara cognatio* during which ancestors were represented by an empty chair. The Roman Feast of 'The Chair of Saint Peter' finds its origin in such a Roman cultural context. It was a way of honoring the apostle Peter – his chair – their ancestor in faith in the Church of Rome. This cultural borrowing would later reveal itself in Roman architecture as well when in the years 609–613, Pope Boniface IV consecrated the pagan temple dedicated to the gods – the Pantheon – as the Christian temple dedicated to the Virgin Mary and the Christian martyrs '*Santa Maria ad Martyres.*' Ten years later in the years 625–628, the old palazzo of the Senate in the Roman Forum was transformed into the Church of Saint Hadrian.

The Passage from Greek to Latin as Liturgical Language

The third and fourth centuries saw a shift in the Roman liturgical language from the use of *koiné* Greek to Latin largely due to North African influence.. Tertullian (+225), for example, had been educated in Rome and could both read and write Greek. But less than thirty or forty years later, a typically educated Carthaginian such as Cyprian could not speak or read Greek and needed someone to translate a letter from Asia Minor written in Greek. We are talking about the years 230 to 240. By then, much of the *Septuagint* (LXX) and the Greek New Testament had been translated into Latin. The translation of the *Septuagint* may well have been initiated by Jews, who like their Christian counterparts in North Africa, could no longer understand Greek. In the third century when the translations were made from Greek into Latin they were done rather slavishly, even reproducing Greek word order and the use of particles – *men* and *de* for example. The use of Latin for scriptural texts is older in Carthage than in Rome. Be that as it may, it was North African theologians such as Tertullian and Augustine who played a leading role in creating the Church's juridical and liturgical terminology that would come to be employed in the Latin West, often borrowing from secular or military vocabulary of the day as mentioned above.

Prior to the third and fourth centuries, Roman Christians as well as Jews used *koiné* Greek as their language in worship since it was the language spoken on the streets and was therefore accessible. The Greek language, however, was to be short-lived in the West as the North African propagation of Latin took hold in Rome and beyond. Consequently, when Roman Christians were no longer able to understand Greek, Church leaders opted for the use of Latin in its worship as a practical means of helping people to pray publicly in a language which they understood. Pope Victor I (+203), an African by birth, made the first attempt to introduce Latin into the liturgy of the Roman Church resulting initially in a bilingual liturgy: Greek for the prayer formularies and Latin for the readings. The two languages continued to be used side by side until the pontificate of Damasus I (+384) when Latin increasingly dominated the landscape and the entire liturgy came to be celebrated in Latin, as a result. The earliest textual evidence we have for the adoption of Latin in the Eucharistic Prayer comes in the years 360–382. Thus, Latin became the official language of the Roman Rite and indeed, of the Roman Catholic Church.[7]

From Rome, the diffusion of Latin spread throughout central and western Europe. Use of liturgical Latin within the Roman Rite continued to develop between the fourth and sixth centuries with the composition of collect prayers during the Mass and the *anaphora* or Eucharistic Prayer. Popes Innocent I (+417), Leo the Great (+461), Gelasius I (+496), Vigilius (+555), and Gregory the Great (+604) were largely responsible for those compositions. In the seventh century due to a second wave of Greek-speaking immigrants, the Roman Liturgy once again became bi-lingual for a fairly brief period of time, using Greek for some of the readings and catechumenal rites.

Today, of course, Latin remains the official language both of the Church and the Roman Rite – an issue clearly misunderstood by many journalists who continually refer to the Pope 'restoring the Latin Mass' when they are, in fact, referring to Benedict's 2007 *Motu Proprio* on the Tridentine Rite. Nonetheless, the early history of liturgical language is instructive as we consider Conciliar debates over Latin and the vernacular which continue to this very day.[8] This question of liturgical language offers one of the earliest examples of what we now call 'inculturation of the Roman Liturgy,' i.e. accommodating the Roman Rite to particular cultural circumstances and needs, producing a liturgy that exhibits and reflects the cultural ethos of that particular celebrating people.

The Roman Rite Takes Shape

The role of papal leadership within liturgical changes extended far beyond the issue of liturgical language. Popes like Damasus and those already mentioned above played significant roles in the evolution of the Roman Rite and in the early composition of liturgical texts. In the late fifth century, Pope Gelasius I introduced the Greek Litany *Kyrie Eleison* into the Roman Rite which replaced the solemn prayers of Intercession. That text was further emended and simplified by Gregory the Great in the following century, offering a shortened form of the *Kyrie* litany. Pope Gregory also placed the Lord's Prayer immediately after the Eucharistic Prayer and before the breaking of the bread, rather than between the *Fractio Panis* and Communion. The new position of the Lord's Prayer allowed the Pope to say the prayer over the consecrated gifts at the altar instead of at the papal throne where he positioned himself at the fraction rite. The *Gloria in Excelsis* first appeared in the Roman Rite during the pontificate of Pope Symmachus (+514) on Sundays at Feasts during Masses at which bishops presided – a custom that was later extended to presbyteral liturgies, as well. The Syrian born Pope Sergius I (+701) introduced the *Agnus Dei* into the Roman Liturgy.

The earliest composition of liturgical texts in the Roman Rite reveals a dynamic not unlike what happened in other rites: a new type of improvisation based on faithful observance of certain canons, guidelines, or principles that were handed on within the local church from one generation to the next. A set of texts was prepared for a specific celebration and then placed in the local archives as a record of the celebration. The one presiding collected the texts into booklets known as *libelli* (*missarum*). A *libellus* contained the presidential prayer texts for a particular Eucharist or a small collection of formulae for more than one Mass. They were originally composed by individuals for their own personal use in the churches they served. Thus, the collections of written liturgical material came into existence, initially intended to serve as a model for other bishops and presbyters as they sought to compose their own liturgical texts.

Gradually, these private liturgical texts were diffused as they came to be copied and adapted and the more authoritative the original author, the more those texts were disseminated. The fourth and fifth centuries witnessed a period of extraordinary Roman liturgical creativity with numerous original texts that were produced during that time – variable texts for the Eucharist; texts for the administration of the Sacraments and for use in the Liturgy of the Hours. Those texts, of course, reflected the literary genius and cultural style of the author and the particular region for which the texts were composed.[9]

The Roman Liturgy of this period can be distinguished for its pure and classical form: 'pure' to indicate that form which existed at Rome before any contact with Gallican or Franco-Germanic elements that arrived in the eighth century; 'classic' because it assimilated the cultural genius of the Romans of that particular epoch – 'the genius of the Roman Rite' that Edmund Bishop spoke about more than one hundred years ago. Bishop spoke of the Roman penchant for 'soberness and sense' which was present in Roman society of the day, whether in poetry or philosophy. The Roman sobriety also implied brevity and a certain practicality.

As the Roman Rite took shape, three types of Roman liturgy can be noted: the solemn papal 'stational' Mass; the presbyteral liturgy celebrated in the Roman *tituli*; and the more simplifed Masses presided over by presybters in rural communities without the help of a choir and perhaps even without the ministry of a deacon. With its lack of ceremonial, this third grouping served as the precursor for Votive Masses and small group celebrations of pilgrims visiting Rome with their bishop or abbot, beginning in the seventh century. Ferial and 'private' Masses would also find their origin in this group.

Be that as it may, even the Papal Stational liturgy itself exhibited that 'noble simplicity' so typical of the Roman cultural genius – at least in its earliest expression.[10] Like Constantinople and Jerusalem, Rome had its own well-developed stational system of worship on feast days, beginning at one church or *statio*, then processing to the designated church for the liturgical celebration. But unlike the elaborate celebrational style of stational liturgy in the East, the Roman model was more reserved. We do not yet find any rubrics for genuflection, incensations or signs of the cross. Only the Bishop of Rome approached the altar to proclaim the Eucharistic Prayer while the presbyters remained in their places – a marked difference when compared to the current practice in Roman concelebration. Similarly, the purpose of the ritual washing of the celebrant's hands during the Roman Eucharist of this period appears to be purely hygenic, with no symbolic reference to his spiritual purification.

The Roman Stational liturgy of this period was, in fact, the local liturgy of the City of Rome from the fifth through the eighth centuries – organized in freedom and making use of the public space afforded it.[11] Because of the laws which did not allow cemeteries within the walls, it was a liturgy celebrated both *In Urbe* and also *Extra Muros* – i.e. both within and outside the walls. The liturgy was highly choreographed with a significant amount of movement, transforming the entire city into sacred space on the feast day. Rome was the only city in the West with such a grand liturgy at the time, so it is not surprising that it came to be a source of imitation for others. In Rome, the seven neighborhoods and centers of *diakonia* each had its own choreographed procession to the designated church where the Bishop of Rome would celebrate the Eucharist. Each of the seven processions was led by the deacon in charge of that particular *diakonia*.

Our use of the term 'Collect' for the Opening Prayer within the Roman Rite of the Eucharist finds its origins in the Roman Stational Liturgy, intended as a conclusion to the entrance procession and its chant. In the Roman Liturgy of that period the processional assembly was called the *Collecta*. In its more developed form, this primary assembly or *collecta* consisted of a prayer *ad collectam* and then the procession moved to the designated stational church. During the procession, psalms and litanies were sung and the term *litania* was often applied to the procession itself. So *collecta* applied to the assembly in movement, and *litania* to the procession. Following the Opening Prayer came the scriptural readings and homily, already attested to in the *Apologia* of Justin in the mid second century. While the

Roman Liturgy originally contained three readings – from the Old Testament; the Pauline corpus; and a Gospel – the readings were reduced to two by the sixth century, divided by a psalm, eliminating the reading from the Hebrew Scriptures.

The Roman Canon offers a perfect example of such elegant and formal language with great use of the subjunctive and inclusion of court gestures such as beating the breast, bows, and genuflections. Eucharistic language still tended to be more indirect than direct. In other words, we don't find much direct language that speaks of 'body'and 'blood' of Christ. Rather we finds terms like 'food and drink,' 'sacrament,' 'gifts of God.' Nor do we find much evidence of what would later be called 'Eucharistic adoration' within the Western Church that would grow in the High Middle Ages, greatly helped by the Scholastic philosophy and theology of Bonaventure, Thomas Aquinas, and others.

The Roman Rite in the Seventh to Twelfth Centuries

The late seventh or early eighth-century *Ordo Romanus Primus* (*OR I*) – part of the collection of the *Ordines romani* – is an important document in helping contemporary liturgical historians to reconstruct the precise ways in which the Church of Rome worshiped in that period and the ways in which Roman court ceremonial was incorporated into the liturgical action. Along with the Medieval ordinals and ceremonials, the *Ordines romani* clearly offer the foundation for what we now call the *General Instruction on the Roman Missal* – a text we will consider in Chapter 4. The oldest of the *ordines*, *OR I* is the first surviving *ordo* of a solemn Papal Mass and of the Eucharist celebrated in Rome in that historical period.[12] Among other things, it provides a very detailed description of the papal stational Mass at *Santa Maria Maggiore* on Easter Sunday morning. There is also a description of the order of the papal procession from the pope's residence at the Lateran, proceeding along the Via Merulana to the designated church for the Eucharistic celebration.

The pope traveled on horseback led by assistants carrying candles, and accompanied by his councilors. At a certain point in the procession, the district notary greeted the pope and informed him: 'In the name of our Lord Jesus Christ, last night there were baptized in the Church of Saint Mary the Theotokos, nn. baby boys and nn. baby girls,' to which the Pope responded: 'Thanks be to God.' When the papal procession arrived at the designated church, the heads of that church were there waiting to greet him along with a choir and other representatives who kissed his hands and feet. The original simplicity and sobriety of the classical Roman Rite was gradually being influenced by Roman court ceremonial. This would also make for wordier and more elaborate prayers with court language employed.

In that same period, a certain process of liturgical amalgamation had already begun north of the Alps, combining elements of the Gallican liturgy with those of the Roman Rite. Why this desire to incorporate Roman elements into the Gallican Rite given such distinct cultural differences? First, there was fairly widespread devotion to the Roman Church because of the tombs of Peter and Paul found there with the concomitant Roman primacy as a result. Bishops and abbots who came to Rome on pilgrimage returned home with copies of Roman liturgical texts and many attempted to imitate the liturgy they had witnessed in Rome. Secondly, there was some confusion and discord among Gallican bishops and abbots on the extensive variations within their worship, so they looked to Rome for leadership. Thirdly, in the eighth century Gallican Emperors like Charlemagne saw the Roman Rite as a key political ingredient in fortifying and unifying the Empire.[13]

Even then, the Roman Rite needed to be adapted in order to make it acceptable in a foreign context. The Gallican ethos was radically different from the Roman – just the opposite of the sobriety and brevity of the Roman Rite. If the Roman liturgy was precise and practical, the Gallican liturgy was poetic and dramatic, prayers were longer and Gallican Missals offered much greater variety in choosing prayers. Indeed, the Gallican Eucharistic Prayer contained many changeable parts for various feasts and seasons throughout the year. And in the spirit of the

Visigoth and Byzantine liturgies, those prayers were customarily addressed to Christ unlike the Roman and North African liturgies which addressed prayers to God the Father through Christ. This was possibly a reflection of the earlier anti-Arian struggle in the North. The Gallican rite also made much greater use of incense and other more sensual liturgical elements. This was the case not only regarding the Eucharist, but in other sacraments, as well. For example, whereas the Roman Ordination Rite limited itself to the laying on of hands and Prayer of Consecration by the Bishop, the Gallican ritual also included an anointing of the hands. The Gallican Rite came to be established in the fourth and fifth centuries so it was hardly an innovation when compared with the Roman Rite.[14]

Be that as it may, this period gradually witnessed a certain decline within liturgical participation in the West. The popular Roman Stational Liturgy fell into disuse after the eighth century and the Mass became increasingly distanced from the people. Latin was retained as a sacral language even at a time when Romance languages were developing and it was no longer intelligible to the masses, thus reinforcing the idea that liturgy was the property of the clergy. Thus, Latin had now become the language of a select educated elite. This led to a new and heightened focus on the person of the celebrating priest. The Roman Canon came to be whispered or spoken *sotto voce* by the celebrant. In the Gallican Rite numerous prayers of a personal and devotional character, called 'apologetic prayers,' were inserted into the liturgy which were to prayed silently by the celebrant in the singular 'I' rather than the plural 'we.' The reception of Holy Communion became ever more the exception than the norm and the Mass as private devotion on the part of clergy became standard fare. Unlike the liturgical diversity and cultural expression that continued in the East, the situation was markedly different in the West and popular devotions increasingly filled the void. Helped by the Pepin the Short (+768) and his anointing as king by Boniface (+754), and the Roman coronation of his son Charlemagne (+814) by Pope Leo III (+816) on Christmas Day 800, cultural diversity and regional expression in worship were sacrificed in favor of a unified Roman Rite that would gradually be imposed on the Western world.

The first example of a written Order of Mass appears in the ninth century. In addition to a Sacramentary, presbyters who presided at an early Medieval liturgy would have also had an additional booklet which contained the outline of the liturgical structure along with a number of apologetic prayers intended for the priest alone. Only in the thirteenth century does the *Ordo missae* come to be standardized.[15]

The tenth century was an especially difficult time for the Roman Rite's capacity to maintain its own distinctly cultural ethos. On the one hand, there was a serious decline within the papacy as far as moral and spiritual integrity were concerned. Beginning around the year 850, election to the papacy fell into the hands of noble Roman families who decided the fate of the Roman Church by appointing their own candidates – often from their own families – to the papacy. What happened in the seventh century with the migration of the Roman Rite toward the north, began to happen in reverse order. Now, the Gallican Rite – itself having been re-worked by the introduction of Roman elements – came to be implanted in Rome, thus creating a new Roman liturgy that was neither Roman nor Gallican in the strict sense of the term. This hybrid form of the Roman Rite was introduced in Rome at the beginning of the tenth century by Emperor Otto I and then by German popes who followed – deliberately chosen because of Ottoman influence. Those popes, of course, had been steeped in the Gallican Rite and were sympathetic to it which made its introduction into Rome a much easier task.

In the eleventh century, Pope Gregory VII (+1085) sought to restore order to the Church in a number of areas including a recovery of the classic Roman Rite. He was especially concerned about unifying liturgical practice in the West under Roman papal authority. For example, he sought to bring Spain into line with the rest of Europe under Roman leadership and worked hard at suppressing the Mozarabic Rite, ultimately without success. Curiously, he did not exhibit a concomitant concern with suppressing the Ambrosian Rite in Milan or the Liturgy of Benevento in southern Italy. Be that as it may, the Gregorian reform attempted to restore the primacy of the Roman Rite in the West but would succeed only in part. Liturgy in the eleventh century was actually quite diverse, much more hybrid than uniform, and it largely remained that way long after Gregory's pontificate had come to an end.

There were various attempts to recover the liturgical participation of the assembly. For example, Gregory VII required people to bring an offering at least for solemn Masses, but that practice would again fall into disuse. By and large, Mass had become a largely private affair – both for clergy and laity, and Gregory – with the most noble of attempts – would not be able significantly to change the direction of the Roman liturgical practice of his day. The Lateran Basilica's twelfth-century *Ordo officorum* decried the fact that the ancient practice of daily Communion during Lent, including Sundays, was not being observed neither by the clergy nor the laity. It thus prescribed Communion of the faithful at least three times each year. Moreover, there were various attempts in the twelfth century to restore the simplicity and sobriety of the Roman Rite, removing those elements that ran contrary to the cultural ethos of the Roman Rite. Once again, however, those attempts at rediscovering the pristine nature of the Roman Rite enjoyed only limited success.

The Roman Rite in the Thirteenth to Sixteenth Centuries

The problems that beset the Roman Rite in this period were varied. Beginning in the eleventh century and especially in the twelfth, the popes increasingly withdrew from the city. People began speaking of the 'papal court' or the *Curia romana* where the Bishop of Rome now resided and from which he received advice on policy. Soon, the pope and his court went their own way, free from the local Church of Rome because it was said that the pope was responsible for 'all the churches.' This, of course, was a far cry from the ecclesiology of the first millennium where the Bishop of Rome had wider jurisdiction in the West precisely and solely because he was Bishop of Rome. Thus, the Curia came to be associated not with the local Roman Church but with the Western Church. Along with his court, the Pope had his own chapel, the *Sancta sanctorum*, where he celebrated the liturgy in isolation, closed off from the clergy and faithful of Rome. This was especially the case with the daily celebration of the Eucharist and the Liturgy of the Hours – celebrated by himself with his court.

On the local parish level, clergy had received little if any theological training. Whatever theological expertise was present in that period was found largely in the monasteries which were often removed from the cities. Language that spoke of the 'fruits of the Sacrifice of the Mass' made the private celebration of the Eucharist increasingly normative, without the presence of the laity. In fact, it was not uncommon in some churches to have Mass celebrated simultaneously at twenty or thirty altars, each Mass offered for one of the living or deceased. To some degree, the Roman Rite in that period had become something of a spiritual business and the emphasis came to focus on 'quantity' (i.e. how many masses can be 'said') rather than on 'quality' (i.e. the one sacrifice of Christ in which the whole Church is united). For example, some priests argued that the grace received from one Mass was equivalent to what was gained from fifteen years of fasting. Not surprisingly, people began to inquire about at what point they needed to arrive at Mass so as not to miss or lose the fruits they might obtain.

By the year 1100, CE, the chalice was no longer offered to the laity at Holy Communion when they did receive because there had already been a significant decline in reception of Holy Communion as far back as the sixth century. Moreover, drinking from the chalice was considered unnecessary and superfluous for those present at Mass. By the year 1200, the offertory procession declined and the bread and wine came to elevated during the Roman Canon. It was within such a context that the *Roman Missal* was introduced and the Order of Mass standardized. In the first millennium, there had been separate liturgical books for the different liturgical ministries: a book for the presider; Book of the Gospels for the deacon; Lectionary for the reader;

Graduale for the choir, etc. But now, the priest celebrant had subsumed all liturgical roles within the Roman Rite under his own ministry. On the one hand, having one book that contained all the liturgical texts was practical and efficient for the Bishop of Rome – both for simple usage in his private chapel and also as the papacy became increasingly itinerant. On the other hand, it no longer mattered whether or not the Roman Rite continued to employ separate books, since the priest or bishop now did everything alone: those in the assembly had become passive spectators. The one-volume *Roman Missal* was also appreciated by the itinerant and mendicant Franciscan Friars as they moved from town to town, and they were among the chief promoters.[16]

Throughout the fourteenth and fifteenth centuries the Roman Rite continued to witness a certain decline both in lay participation and theological/historical understanding of its original ethos, and liturgical abuses around its celebration – often linked with superstitions and monetary offerings – were not unknown. In fact, reverence for the reserved sacrament became more important than eating and drinking the Lord's body and blood. This was so much the case that the Feast of *Corpus Christi*, where the reserved sacrament was carried in procession through the streets of many towns and cities in Western Europe, became more important than the feast of Easter! Thus, with the arrival of Martin Luther and other reformers of the sixteenth century, their criticisms were not without foundation. It is important that the Council of Trent (1545–1563) be viewed in this light since that Council both attempted to respond to the critique of the Reformers while at the same time face squarely the abuses that plagued the sixteenth-century Catholic Church – including liturgical abuses – in its celebration of the Roman Rite.

The Tridentine Reform of the Roman Liturgy

Pope Pius IV established a liturgical commission to reform the Roman Rite – a task which was unable to be undertaken during the Council itself, and the commission was expanded with the election of Pius V two years later in 1566. There was much work to be done not only in revising the liturgical calendar to give greater attention to the liturgical seasons, but also in the revision and elimination of certain liturgical texts as well as liturgical ceremonies themselves. Despite common impressions of that Council, a fundamental goal of the post-Tridentine liturgical commission was to recover the pristine liturgical style of the Patristic Church under the papal leadership and authority.

We can distinguish three characteristics of the Tridentine reform of the Roman Rite. First, there was the centralization of authority organized under the Pope and the Roman Curia which made the liturgy of the papal court normative. This centralization was a response to the Protestant Reformation, eliminating all innovations introduced by individuals and also correcting liturgical abuses. It was for this reason that the Roman Congregation for Sacred Rites was founded in 1588 – both to foster liturgical unity and monitor the celebration of the Roman Rite for the Western Church.

A second characteristic was an emphasis on rubrics as a practical means of maintaining uniformity throughout the universal Church. This led to a new mentality: rubricism had moral and juridical consequences with concerns over the validity or invalidity of a Mass. Rubrics that were once descriptive guidelines had become obligatory norms.

A third characteristic was the pastoral dimension. Although the Council of Trent is often described in restrictive terms as a council that was opposed to change, it had a fundamentally pastoral scope. This was evidenced by significant discussion on topics such as offering the chalice to the laity at Communion and use of vernacular languages in celebrating the Roman Rite.[17] In principle, those two items were not flatly rejected, but rather the bishops opted for prudence, arguing that it was an inopportune time to introduce those changes and more catechesis would be needed. There were, in fact, some exceptions, or what we might call 'liturgical experimentation' in the years immediately after the Tridentine Council. Communion under both forms was authorized for Germany in 1564 by Pope Pius IV and the Archbishop of Prague granted a similar concession for his own archdiocese in 1573 in response to a request which came from the Jesuit college there. A return to such Patristic customs would be short-lived however, and they had been discontinued by the early seventeenth century.[18]

At the heart of the Tridentine reform was a desire to return to the classic Roman Rite, among other things, to show Protestant reformers its great value. With the promulgation of the Roman Breviary of Pius V in 1568 and the *Roman Missal* of 1570, and with the founding of the Congregation for Sacred Rites in 1588, a clear direction was given for liturgical uniformity under Roman leadership. The Tridentine reform of the Roman Rite was to be implemented universally, with the obvious exception of those churches with special permission to use their own rites such as the Ambrosian Rite in Milan and the Mozarabic Rite in Spain, and religious orders such as the Dominicans which could prove the antiquity of their respective rites. In order to continue celebrating in a particular rite, it needed to be demonstrated that the rite had been in use for more than two hundred years.

Thus the Tridentine celebration of the Roman Rite would hold sway for four hundred years, until the advent of the Second Vatican Council (1962–1965). However, we must not be naive in thinking that the Tridentine liturgical reforms were not also met with resistance in certain regions. France, for example, refused to accept the Tridentine liturgical norms of Roman centralization until well into the nineteenth century. And in neighboring Germany, the Diocese of Münster waited until 1890 to implement the Missal of Pius V – 320 years after its promulgation!

Conclusion

As we have seen in this first chapter, the Roman Rite evolved and changed over the centuries, often for pastoral reasons, accommodating and adapting to the cultural and practical needs of the Church. Thus recent appeals to the unchanging Roman Rite that has been in continuous usage until the Second Vatican Council would appear to be disingenuous. Indeed, while maintaining the 'substantial unity of the Roman Rite' as *Sacrosanctum concilium* demanded, if we are to remain consistent with those who have gone before us, the Church must continually work quite intentionally at contextualizing and incarnating that Roman Rite within the diverse cultural contexts in which it is lived and celebrated. In the next chapter, we shall explore the continued evolution of the Roman Rite as evidenced in the liturgical reforms of the Second Vatican Council.

Notes

1   Edmund Bishop, 'The Genius of the Roman Rite,' in *Liturgica Historica: Papers on the Liturgy and Religious Life of the Western Church* (Oxford: Clarendon Press, 1918, 1962), 19.
2   Bishop, 2.
3   See Edward Foley, *From Age to Age: How Christians Have Celebrated the Eucharist* (Collegeville: The Liturgical Press, 2008), 85–86.
4   David Ulansey, *The Origins of the Mithraic Mysteries: Cosmology and Salvation in the Ancient World* (Oxford: Oxford University Press, 1989), 4.
5   *I Apologia* 66.
6   See Robert Turcan, *The Cults of the Roman Empire* (Oxford: Blackwell, 1996), 114–121.
7   See Enrico Cattaneo, *Il Culto Cristiano in Occidente* (Roma: CLV, 1992), 97–113.
8   See Keith F. Pecklers, *Dynamic Equivalence: The Living Language of Christian Worship* (Collegeville: The Liturgical Press, 2003).
9   See Éric Palazzo, *A History of Liturgical Books From the Beginning to the Thirteenth Century* (Collegeville: The Liturgical Press/Pueblo, 1998), 35–38.
10 For an excellent treatment on the Stational Liturgy see John F. Baldovin, *The Urban Character of Christian Worship: The Origins, Development, and Meaning of Stational Liturgy* (Rome: Pont. Institutum Studiorum Orientalium, 1987).
11 See Antoine Chavasse, *La liturgie de la ville de Rome du V au VIII siècle* (Roma: Studia Anselmiana 112, 1993), 13–26.

12 See Palazzo, *A History of Liturgical Books*, 173–177; see also Joanne M. Pierce, 'The Evolution of the *Ordo Missae* in the Early Middle Ages,' in Lizette Larson-Miller, *Medieval Liturgy* (New York: Garland Publishing Inc., 1997), 3–24.

13 See Éric Palazzo, *Liturgie et société au Moyen Age* (Aubier, 2000).

14 See Matthieu Smyth, *'Ante Altaria' Les rites antiques de la messe domincale en Gaule, en Espagne et en Italie du Nord* (Paris: Cerf, 2007).

15 Joanne M. Pierce, 'Evolution of the *Ordo missae*,' in Lizette Larson-Miller, *Medieval Liturgy* (New York: Garland Publishing, Inc., 1997), 5–6.

16 Burkhard Neunheuser, *Storia della liturgia attraverso le epoche culturali* (Roma: CLV, 1999), 123–131.

17 See Herman A.P. Schmidt, S.J., *Liturgie et Langue Vulgaire: Le problème de la langue liturgique chez les premiers Réformateurs et au Concile de Trente* (Roma: Analecta Gregoriana 53, 1950).

18 See Nathan D. Mitchell, 'Reforms, Protestant and Catholic,' in Geoffrey Wainright and Karen B. Westerfield Tucker, *The Oxford History of Christian Worship* (Oxford: Oxford University Press, 2006), 337.

Recovering Tradition

2

The Conciliar Reforms of Vatican II and the Post-Conciliar Liturgical Renewal

Introduction

Having considered the historical evolution of the Roman Rite in the first chapter, we now look at how the Second Vatican Council endeavored to recover the roots of that tradition. As we have already seen, the pure and classical Roman Rite was found in the fifth to the eighth centuries. As the Roman Rite continued to grow in the Middle Ages, Gallican and other non-Roman liturgical elements continued to be added – numerous apologetic prayers of the priest, for example, asking for his personal sanctification; increased incensations and more elaborate processions. Even the Nicene Creed itself was not originally known in the Roman Rite; it was introduced only in the year 1014 at the request of the German King Henry II when he came to Rome to be crowned Holy Roman Emperor by Pope Benedict VIII (+1024) and asked that the Creed might be sung during his coronation Mass. There was also the problem of a loss of integrity regarding the calendar of the liturgical year. Sundays – even during Advent and Lent – came to be reserved to keep the memorial of saints, often listing several on the calendar for the same day. Apart from the Council's desire to restore the Roman Rite to its pristine origins, there was a concomitant desire to recover the participation of the liturgical assembly which had diminished significantly over the centuries.

As noted in the first chapter, restoring the noble simplicity of the Roman Rite had already been attempted at the Council of Trent (1545–63); at the Synod of Pistoia held in 1786,[1] and even more in 1832 when Prosper Guéranger re-founded the French Benedictine monastery of Solesmes which had been suppressed during the French Revolution. When Guéranger came on the scene, French resistence to the Tridentine liturgical reforms continued to hold sway and ninety of the 139 dioceses in France had their own distinct liturgies. Indeed, some dioceses such as Versailles and Beauvais had as many as nine Breviaries and Missals.[2] Thus, as an antidote to such non-Roman liturgical diversity, Guéranger sought to assist the French Church in returning to its true foundations through a proper celebration of the Tridentine Roman Rite.

The twentieth-century liturgical movement made its own important contribution to restoring the classic Roman Rite. Unlike Guéranger whose research on the Roman liturgy was limited to medieval liturgical books, liturgical pioneers on both sides of the Atlantic returned to Patristic foundations, working in tandem with proponents of the biblical, patristic, and ecumenical movements in what came to be known as *ressourcement* – a return to the sources. It is precisely such collaboration with those other movements for Church renewal that helps us to understand the liturgical movement's success. The Pauline doctrine of the Church as the Mystical Body of Christ recovered at Tübingen in the nineteenth century offered the theological grounding for the movement's agenda.

At the dawn of the twentieth century, Pope Pius X's *Motu proprio* of 1903 *'Tra le sollecitudini'* spoke of the liturgy as 'the true and indispensable source for the Christian life – a principle which became the liturgical movements's *magna carta*:

> Since we have very much at heart that the true Christian spirit be revived in all possible ways and that it be maintained among all the faithful, it is above all necessary to provide for the holiness and dignity of sacred places where precisely the faithful gather to draw this spirit at its primary and indispensable source, that is, active participation in the sacred mysteries and in the public and solemn prayer of the Church.[3]

This theme was further developed in Pius XII's 1947 Encyclical *Mediator Dei* – the first papal encyclical on the Sacred Liturgy. *Mediator Dei*, of course, was not exactly a *carte blanche* approval of the liturgical movement's agenda. On the contrary, even as the Pope did allow for certain adaptations and concessions (e.g., on the use of the vernacular in certain rites), he was also quite critical of some aspects of the liturgical movement and advised caution in the way of proceeding. Nonetheless, pioneers of the liturgical movement interpreted *Mediator Dei* positively as a certain ratification of their efforts, and continued to promote the sacred liturgy as that 'true and indispensable source' for Christian living – a concept that would remain foundational for Vatican II's Constitution on the Sacred Liturgy.

Speaking of the Church as the Mystical Body of Christ together with the liturgy as the Church's 'primary and indispensable source' implied and indeed demanded an intimate link between worship and social concern. It was fitting, then, that the liturgical movement was founded in 1909 at a Catholic labor congress in Belgium, drawing on both the *Motu Proprio* of Pius X and on Leo XII's social encyclical *Rerum novarum*. Equally significant is the fact that the movement was founded by a former labor chaplain turned Benedictine monk, Lambert Beauduin.

As a response to *Mediator Dei,* Pius XII established a secret commission for liturgical reform on 28 May 1948, chaired by the Prefect of the Sacred Congregation of Rites, Cardinal Clement Micara, which continued its work for twelve years until it was dissolved in 1960. Known as the 'Pian Commission,' its contribution was quite significant and pastoral in scope. Very soon, its efforts bore fruit in very concrete results: an abbreviation of the required Eucharistic fast from the midnight before receiving Communion to just one hour prior. This led to the possibility of celebrating Mass in the evening as well. The Commission was also responsible for the restoration of the Easter Vigil in 1951 and then the reform of the Holy Week liturgies in 1955. While the work of the Pian Commission is largely unknown, it offers an important historical piece as we attempt to understand the liturgical reforms of Vatican II. Here was a liturgical commission already established by Pope Pius XII in 1948 – a full fourteen years before the first session of the Council took place.

Sacrosanctum concilium and the Liturgical Reforms of Vatican II

On 4 December 2008 the universal Church celebrated the forthy-fifth anniversary of the promulgation of the Second Vatican Council's Liturgy Constitution *Sacrosanctum concilium*, which the Council bishops approved with an astounding majority: 2,147 in favor and 4 opposed, with very few changes from what had originally been proposed. This represented a great break-through despite last-minute attempts in certain circles of the Roman Curia to sideline the process in favor of a rubrical, centralized, and rigidly immutable Roman liturgy celebrated in Latin. Thus, the Constitution was solemnly approved by Pope Paul VI – the first decree to be promulgated by the Ecumenical Council. As has already been noted, at the heart of that document was a return to the solid foundations inherent within the pure and classical Roman Rite, all of which came to be rediscovered in the work of the liturgical movement and, indeed, the wider movement of *ressourcement* theology, which paved the way for the Council as evidenced in the work of the Pian Commission discussed above.

It would, of course, prove impossible to reconstruct the Roman Rite of an earlier epoch since what we call the Roman Rite today is actually a hybrid of various elements and accretions which reformed the Rite over the centuries. Critics of the Conciliar liturgical reform have accused its architects of liturgical archeology – trying to reconstruct the early medieval Roman liturgy while failing to take account of the ways the Roman Rite has grown organically over time.[4] In other words, the myth of the fourth century as the 'golden age' of the catechumenate, or the fifth to eighth centuries as the 'golden age' of the Roman Rite is just that, a myth. And the liturgy must always be contextualized to the pastoral needs of the particular age in which it is being celebrated.

Vatican II was, in fact, very much aware of the pastoral and cultural context in which it was convoked. It was well aware of change in the world – more than any of the twenty ecumenical councils that preceded it. Indeed, it had emerged within the complex social context of the Cuban Missile Crisis, a rise in Communism, and military dictatorships in various corners of the globe. President John F. Kennedy had been assassinated only twelve days prior to the promulgation of *Sacrosanctum concilium*.[5] Despite those global crises, however, the Council generally viewed the world positively and with a certain degree of optimism. The credibility of the Church's message would necessarily depend on its capacity to reach far beyond the confines of the Catholic ghetto into the marketplace – into non-Christian and indeed, non-religious spheres.[6] It is important that the liturgical reforms be examined within such a framework.

The Council's Preparatory Commission of over sixty-five members and thirty consultants hailing from twenty-five countries and five continents demonstrated the international breadth and scope of such a working body. The Commission prepared a schema which included areas that required both theological reinterpretation as well as ritual revision: the mystery of the liturgy in relation to the Church's life and common witness; the Eucharistic celebration with particular attention to presbyteral concelebration; the Liturgy of the Hours; sacraments and sacramentals; revision of the liturgical calendar; the use of Latin; liturgical formation both for clergy and laity; liturgical participation; linguistic adaptations to different cultures and peoples; the simplification of liturgical vestments; sacred music and art. The schema attempted to treat the fullness of the Church's liturgical life and after several drafts and emendations, the final text was presented to the Council Fathers as the Liturgy Constitution. It was the first item on the agenda as it was considered a fairly unproblematic subject which could be treated expeditiously. That was not the case.

Aside from tensions over the content of the document itself, there were also internal conflicts. At the beginning of the Council, Father Annibale Bugnini, who served as Secretrary of

Pius XII's secret liturgical commission and was, in fact, the chief architect of the Conciliar liturgical reforms, was seen as too progressive by the Roman Curia. So on 21 October 1962 he was removed as Secretary of the Preparatory Commission by the newly appointed Prefect of the Congregation for Sacred Rites, Cardinal Arcadio Larraona, C.M.F. Larroana, a very conservative canon lawyer, was the *ex officio* President of the Preparatory Liturgical Commission. Among other things, he believed that Bugnini was the main protagonist in the Preparatory Commission's aversion to Latin in the liturgy. Bugnini was replaced by a staff member in the Congregation, Father Ferdinando Antonelli, O.F.M. Bugnini would later be rehabilitated by Pope Paul VI in 1964, when he was named Secretary of the International *Consilium* charged with implementing the reforms.

Conciliar discussions on the proposed liturgical document ran from 22 October until 13 November 1962 during fifteen general congregations lasting about fifty hours with 328 oral interventions and 297 written proposals.[7] *Sacrosanctum concilium* clearly established the general principles and norms that were to be observed in reforming the Roman liturgy: 'The rites should be marked by a noble simplicity; they should be short, clear, and unencumbered by useless repetitions; they should be within the people's power of comprehension and as a rule not require much explanation.'[8] It was precisely 'noble simplicity' which characterized the Roman Rite as it grew from the fifth to the eighth centuries before it came into contact with the more dramatic, poetic, and verbose Gallican Rite. Even more explicit is what is contained in Number 50:

> The rites are to be simplified, due care being taken to preserve their substance which, with the passage of time, came to be duplicated, or were added with little advantage, are now to be discarded; other elements which have suffered injury through accidents of history are now to be restored to their vigor which they held in the days of the holy Fathers, as may be useful and necessary.

The Liturgy Constitution reveals three fundamental bases in his reform of the Roman Rite: first, a historical consciousness and desire to return to the sources. Thanks to its contact with the biblical, patristic, and ecumenical movements, the liturgical movement recovered the Church's foundational liturgical documents which we saw in the first chapter. Indeed, that historical consciousness had a huge effect on the Council's agenda in reforming the Roman Rite.

Second, there was a recovery of liturgical theology and spirituality – that the heart of Christian liturgy is always the paschal mystery of Christ. This included a renewed understanding of ecclesiology as foundational for Christian worship since it is in and through the liturgy that the Christian community is more fully in communion with the mystery of Christ and the Church, and is more clearly able to make that communion manifest in the world through the living out of its worship in daily life. This link between liturgy and ecclesiology is a direct result of the sacramental view of the Church as Christ's mystical body with the liturgy at the heart of the Church's life and mission.

Third, there was a strong pastoral desire to promote 'full and active participation,' drawing the faithful out of their passivity into the action of celebrating the Roman Rite. We read at Article 14:

> Mother Church earnestly desires that all the faithful should be led to that full, conscious, and active participation in liturgical celebrations which is demanded by the very nature of the liturgy ... In the restoration and promotion of the sacred liturgy, this full and active participation by all the people is the aim to be considered before all else; for it is the primary and indispensable source from which the faithful are to derive their true Christian spirit; and therefore pastors of souls must zealously strive to achieve it, by means of the necessary instruction, in all their pastoral work.

However, it would be naive to think that all the Council bishops were on the same page when it came to the subject of *actuosa participatio.* Cardinal James McIntyre of Los Angeles sent shock waves through the Vatican basilica when he exclaimed during his intervention: 'Active Participation of the faithful in the Mass is nothing but a distraction.' The phrase had apparently come from an article published by the French Philosopher Jacques Maritain who argued that religion was essentially an act of contemplation. Of course, Church Fathers like Ambrose and Augustine had argued just the opposite: that the Platonic notion of the good as one's final end was, in fact, not the Christian idea of religion at all. Maritain later corrected himself in a subsequent article – a text of which McIntyre's theological advisor clearly had not seen. What was most surprising to the gathered bishops was that McIntyre's comment had come so late in the discussion, suggesting that he actually had not been following the numerous important interventions on the subject which had been made prior to his own.[9]

The notion of 'full and active participation,' in fact, was based on the Pauline theology of a common baptismal priesthood in Jesus Christ – a doctrine that would come to be articulated in the Council's Dogmatic Constitution on the Church *Lumen Gentium.* This liturgical participation was not one option among many, but rather the 'right and duty' of all Christians by virtue of their baptism. Thus, the Council argued that to facilitate such participation, the rites should be accessible and unencumbered, within the grasp of people's comprehension; use of the vernacular is encouraged along with greater recognition of the role of the laity in exercising the different liturgical ministries. The faithful were to receive Communion at the Masses they attended – Communion consecrated at that particular Mass rather than taken from the tabernacle. The Council affirmed that such participation at the moment of Holy Communion might even include the giving of the chalice to the lay faithful – at least on special occasions – depending on local norms and with the permission of the local Ordinary.

The Constitution on the Sacred Liturgy gave attention to the importance of scripture – fruit of the twentieth century biblical movement whose influence was felt also within the liturgical movement. Article 24, for example, notes the importance of Sacred Scripture within the liturgical action: 'to achieve this restoration, progress, and adaptation of the sacred liturgy, it is essential to promote that warm and living love for scripture to which the venerable tradition of both eastern and western rites gives testimony.' Article 35 encourages more reading from the scripture during liturgical celebrations and calls for the restoration of liturgical preaching whose content is drawn mainly 'from scriptural and liturgical sources.' Article 51 states: 'The treasures of the bible are to be opened up more lavishly, so that richer fare may be provided for the faithful at the table of God's Word,' while the following number re-affirms the importance of the homily within the liturgical action, stating that it should not be omitted on Sundays and feasts 'except for a serious reason.'

The Prayer of the Faithful was also restored for Sundays and feast days, in which the liturgical assembly prays for the needs of the Church, for political leaders, for the oppressed and needy, for all people, and for the salvation of the world.[10] Article 90 affirms the importance of recovering the Divine Office as the public prayer of the Church – a source of devotion and nourishment in living out the Christian life. In all of this, we see the Council's desire to recover the unity between Word and Sacrament – between the table of God's Word and the table of the holy Eucharist. Prior to Vatican II, while Catholics would have readily affirmed the real presence of Christ in the Eucharist, there was little understanding of the presence of Christ in the holy Word. *Sacrosanctum concilium* sets the record straight: 'Christ is present in his Word, since it is he himself who speaks when the holy scriptures are read in the Church.'[11]

Those major themes that marked the pre-Conciliar liturgical movement came to play a significant role in the shaping of the Liturgy Constitution, and then in the implementation of the reforms under the leadership of the international *Consilium*. Thus, it is important that Vatican II be seen as much the ratification of the efforts of the liturgical movement – already evidenced in *Mediator Dei* and the Pian Commission of 1948 – as it was a point of departure for the liturgical renewal that has led us to the present day. The Liturgy Constitution strikes a careful balance between historical and theological foundations, between 'sound tradition and legitimate progress.' In many respects, it was a *via media* – a compromise document that attempted to appease both conservative and progressive camps. For example, despite popular misconceptions, the Council did not completely abolish Latin. Indeed, the translations of the post-Conciliar liturgical texts (prayers, readings, and blessings) begin with the original Latin text (called the '*editio typica*' or 'typical edition') from which the text is carefully translated into Latin. This is what we shall be exploring in the fifth chapter as we consider the forthcoming English translation of the Third Edition of the Latin *editio typica* of the *Roman Missal*.

At the same time, however, *Sacrosanctum concilium* was much more than a *via media*. In some cases it called for a complete revision of liturgical books and not a mere superficial editing of what was present in the Tridentine liturgy.[12] And while the Constitution did not use the term 'inculturation,' it does acknowledge the need to allow for 'legitimate variations and adaptation to different groups, regions, and peoples, especially in mission lands.'[13] Several paragraphs later, the text is even more forthright: 'In some places and circumstances, however, an even more radical adaptation of the liturgy is needed.'[14] In other words, it may not be enough to simply adapt the Roman Rite to particular cultures and circumstances.

The principle of collegiality among bishops was clearly operative in the Constitution: liturgical matters pertaining to the local church were best dealt with by episcopal conferences or even by diocesan bishops themselves.[15] Such liturgical decentralization was justified by the fact that the diocesan bishop is empowered to shepherd that local church and not merely serve as a sort of district representative or middle manager. Thus the diocesan bishop or episcopal conference should have the authority to make appropriate liturgical decisions that pertain to the particular local church in question.[16] Nonetheless, an underlying tension around the issue of collegiality held sway during Council sessions, largely between bishops and cardinals of the Roman Curia who were suspicious of extending authority to episcopal conferences, as opposed to diocesan bishops whose pastoral experience made them less threatened by such decentralization.

That division between the Roman Curia and diocesan bishops is well demonstrated in the recently published book by Archbishop Piero Marini, the former Papal Master of Ceremonies. In that text, entitled *A Challenging Reform: Realizing the Vision of the Liturgical Renewal*,[17] Marini argues that resistance to the liturgical changes was largely centered in the Congregation for Divine Worship which sought to maintain a monopoly on the liturgical reform itself and approval of liturgical texts, both out of a fear of losing control of the process and based on a conservative theology that distrusted the reforms of the Council. This tension was made most explicit in a 1964 letter signed by all the Bishop members of the French Liturgical Commission on 7 February and sent to several dicasteries of the Roman Curia. The letter addressed the subject of liturgical translation as an issue of collegiality:

> The Council did not decide that the Assemblies would propose this or that concession for the vernacular to be approved by the Holy See … Neither did the Council state that the bishops' conferences would submit translations for approval by the Apostolic See; it agreed that the translations would be approved by the bishops' conferences, that is all … People are saying that just two months after its promulgation, that the Constitution is beaten in the breach, that the decisions made by episcopal assemblies may be effectively neutralized by the Roman Curia, that the role of the bishops' assemblies is being undermined at the very moment of its establishment by the Council, and that the decisions of the Council are being contested even before the Council has finished.[18]

The Work of the International *Consilium* and Implementation of the Conciliar Liturgical Reforms

If members of the Preparatory Commission and the Council Fathers themselves found their task to be daunting, the greater challenge was yet to come. The reforms would need to be implemented and the universal Church would have to be formed and catechized in a new worship style and language. Thus the International *Consilium* was formed by Pope Paul VI in January, 1964, with Cardinal Giacomo Lercaro of Bologna as President and Annibale Bugnini as Secretary. Commenting on those appointments, Archishop Marini writes:

> The discreet appointment of Lercaro and Bugnini ... was essential for the success of the reform. These appointments made by Paul VI demonstrated not only the open-mindedness on the Pope's part but also a fair degree of courage. Lercaro enjoyed greater prestige internationally than in Italy. Within the Roman Curia and beyond, he was often seen as being too progressive, both in terms of his politics and his liturgical views. As for Bugnini, his appointment was truly a vindication, since it was only one year before that he had been sidelined by the Curia. From that moment on, he would remain at the helm of the liturgical reform of Vatican II until 1975, when the Congregation for Divine Worship was restructured.[19]

From its inception, the *Consilium* was charged with the task of revising existing liturgical books so that they were in harmony with the directives of the Council. Even more important was the editing and revision of the Latin post-Conciliar liturgical books which would then be translated into vernacular languages by regional commissions. The *Consilium* also worked on composing new liturgical texts such as three new Eucharistic Prayers in 1968. Despite its efforts, however, ongoing tensions remained within the Congregation for Divine Worship which gradually limited the *Consilium*'s authority and also impeded the liturgical authority of episcopal conferences as seen above in the French. Bishops' Memorandum.

Archbishop Marini attributes part of this tension to two conflicting systems that do not easily integrate with one another. The Roman Curia is that which was created after the Council of Trent. The forebear of our Congregation for Divine Worship and the Discipline of the Sacraments, for example, was the

Congregation for Sacred Rites founded in 1588 to implement the Tridentine liturgical decrees as we saw in the first chapter. That Council produced no liturgy constitution like *Sacrosanctum Concilium*, rather it was the task of the Congregation of Sacred Rites to give the needed liturgical direction. Prior to Trent, of course, Roman congregations did not exist, but dicasteries such as the Congregation of Sacred Rites were founded precisely to deal with order and uniformity in the post-Tridentine Church. Nowhere in the Tridentine Missal of Pius V is reference made to the 'People of God.' Rather the problem of the day was unity – liturgical unity and the unity of the Church, especially in light of the Protestant Reformation. Not surprisingly, therefore, the emphasis was on a common language, fixed rubrics, norms to be observed by everyone, and virtually no room for adaptation. The liturgy, like the Roman Congregations themselves, was shaped by the same circumstances.[20]

Both the *Consilium* and Congregation for Divine Worship existed to facilitate implementation of the liturgical reforms of the Second Vatican Council on the international level, but the greater challenge would be implementation on the local and regional levels. For example, the Holy See initially found it difficult to understand why the Spanish-speaking churches of Latin America could not use the same vernacular liturgical books as the Church in Spain. Linguistic issues – not to mention historic and cultural ones – soon made it clear that there were too many variances to support just one translation in Castilian Spanish from the Latin *editio typica*.

Reflecting on the implementation of the Conciliar reforms in *America* magazine, veteran liturgical scholar Robert Taft, S.J. of the Pontifical Oriental Institute in Rome, delineated three areas which the reform did not treat well: the process of Christian Initiation; the Liturgy of the Hours; and Communion from the Tabernacle. Taft underscores the irony that one of Pius X's most celebrated and enduring reforms – the lowering of the age for first holy Communion from adolescence to the age of reason – had the unfortunate effect of shifting the time of first Communion before Confirmation, and in the process making first Confession precede first Communion, thereby destroying the age-old sequence of the rites of Christian Initiation. While there have been attempts to restore that ancient order of Christian Initiation in several dioceses and regions, most notably in England and Scotland, the results have been uneven.

Taft's second point deals with the reformed Liturgy of the Hours, which he remarks, is not 'liturgy' at all but rather a breviary or book of prayers. Even in its reformed state, it remains largely a private and clerical activity rather than a prayer of and by the whole Church. Third, despite the injunction of Pope Benedict XIV in 1742 to stop distributing Holy Communion from the tabernacle, it continues to be normative in many parishes to over-consecrate or to consecrate a sufficient number of hosts to last for the week. Church legislation, of course, has never made provision for distribution of Holy Communion during Mass from the tabernacle. The tabernacle is to be reserved for *viaticum* and for Eucharistic devotion. Technically speaking, even Communion for the sick and homebound should be taken from the altar of a given Eucharist and not from the tabernacle.

How then are we to interpret our post-Conciliar liturgical history as it has unfolded these past forty-five years? It has been argued that in the period immediately after the Council too much happened too quickly. Bishops returned home from the Council enthusiastic to put into practice the new liturgical norms and principles, but few were sufficiently prepared to lead their dioceses in implementing the reforms. Complex Latin liturgical texts were translated into English and other vernacular languages expeditiously, producing an English edition of the *Roman Missal* in only four years. The Church in the English-speaking world breathed the *bon aire* of liturgical experimentation with home masses, folk masses, home-grown Eucharistic Prayers, and even liturgical texts sung to the tune of Bob Dylan's 'Blowin' in the Wind!'

Much of the criticism against the liturgical experimentation of the 1960s and 1970s was not without justification, and mistakes were made. Conservative scholars like the German liturgical historian Klaus Gamber referred to that time as a period of 'complete liturgical anarchy.'[21] While other liturgical scholars might be a bit more muted in their assessment of those years immediately after the Council, few would contend that the period was unproblematic. Indeed, those of us who are old enough to remember could tell stories about places where all sorts of 'liturgical experiments' were conducted under the guise of 'creativity' – normally registering little success. But as Cardinal John Henry Newman remarked after Vatican I, every Church council has been followed by a period of turmoil and unrest. It would be enough to think of the aftermath of Nicea and Chalcedon, but even the Council of Trent did not succeed in gaining unanimous adherence to its decrees as already mentioned.

As we look back at work of the International *Consilium* and the implementation of the liturgical reforms at the local level, it was carried out as best as was possible at the time and we are in a far better place today liturgically than we were back in 1963 when *Sacrosanctum concilium* was promulgated. Conservative critics point to the numerous flaws in the first English translation of the *Missal* of Paul VI – a point on which few liturgical scholars would disagree. Moreover, we need to remember that the liturgical renewal has only recently celebrated its forty-fifth anniversary. Indeed, a mere four decades are but a brief moment in our tradition when one considers that it has been a millennium and a half since we last undertook vernacularization in the late fourth century, when Latin came to be introduced into the Roman Rite.

The 'Extraordinary Form of the Roman Rite'

Regardless of how one assesses the post-Conciliar liturgical renewal, however, the fact of the matter is that the Roman Catholic Church became increasingly polarized in the late twentieth century and much of this polarization has focused upon the liturgy itself. A small but vocal and influential group that was critical of the *'novus ordo'* in the years following the Council lobbied for a return to the usage of the pre-Conciliar (1962) *Missale Romanum*. In fact, only seven years after the promulgation of *Sacrosanctum concilium,* Pope Paul VI granted an indult to elderly priests in 1970 who preferred to continue celebrating the pre-Conciliar rite in private.

The schism launched by Archbishop Marcel Lefebvre and his traditionalist movement led Pope John Paul II to make several overtures at reconciliation. Indeed, during his pontificate, two indults were granted for a limited use of the Tridentine Rite – first in 1984 with the document *Quattuor Abhinc Annos,* issued by the Congregation for Divine Worship and the Discipline of the Sacraments. Four years later Pope John Paul issued his own Apostolic Lettter *'Ecclesia Dei'* on 2 July 1988, which established the *Ecclesia Dei* Commission in order to 'facilitate full ecclesial communion'with the followers of Archbishop Marcel Lefebvre who wished to remain within the Catholic Church. But with the *Motu proprio Summorum Pontificum* of Pope Benedict XVI on 7 July 2007, the pre-Conciliar rite received a new status. No longer restricted to limited usage, the 1962 Rite could now be celebrated throughout the universal Church *ad libitum.* Indeed, in the Holy Father's letter to bishops that accompanied the *Motu proprio,* he suggests that the two forms of the usage of the Roman Rite can be 'mutually enriching.'[22]

As Bishop of Rome and universal pastor, the Holy Father himself stated that he granted this universal permission for wider use of the Tridentine Rite out of love for the Church and concern for that small minority of disenfranchised Catholics who felt excluded by the *novus ordo.* In the practical order, however, the *Motu proprio* has been read as victory by the Church's conservative wing and a positive step in correcting or even negating the Council's agenda despite the Pope's stating the contrary. The Italian professor Nicola Bux, for example, has argued that the *Motu Proprio* actually offers a 'step forward' for the Church – part of a 'new liturgical movement.'[23]

As has been brought to light in the months after the document's promulgation, there are some significant ecclesiological and pastoral problems with the document which were not anticipated prior to its promulgation. The widely publicized reaction both in Jewish and Christian circles to the Prayer for the Jews in the Good Friday Liturgy as found in the 1962 *Missal* which asks that God 'lift the veil from their eyes so that they may come to accept Jesus Christ as the savior' presented a serious problem needing attention. Allowing the continued usage of that 1962 prayer would have obviously offered a mixed message in what Vatican II Conciliar theology states about Jews, as evidenced in the Council's decree *Nostra Aetate* and also in the work of the Vatican's dialogue with Jews in these post-Conciliar years.

While some conservative organizations and seminaries are now celebrating the 1962 rite with a certain regularity, and places where it is being celebrated are drawing crowds of young people often out of curiosity for experiencing what they never knew growing up, I do not believe that the 'Extraordinary Form of the Roman Rite' poses any significant threat to the Conciliar liturgy or its ongoing renewal. Among other things, few priests are capable of celebrating the pre-Conciliar rite although there are various attempts at training seminarians and young priests to do so through short courses and DVDs. More importantly, statistics show a very small number of Catholics actually desirous of the Tridentine Rite. The Second Vatican Council has set us on a path from which the Church cannot and will not turn back, especially evident within the full breadth of its liturgical life. And there is much work that remains to be done by way of implementing the Council's liturgical vision. When I published my history of the US liturgical movement, I deliberately entitled the book *The Unread Vision*,[24] taking the phrase from T.S. Eliot's poem 'Ash Wednesday:' 'Redeem the unread vision in the higher dream.' My point was that the rich theological, ecclesiological vision of the liturgy as envisaged by the pioneers of the twentieth-century liturgical movement come to full stature in the Second Vatican Council has yet to be 'read'– understood, and fully implemented.

The Liturgical Renewal Forty-Five Years On: Finding a Way Forward

Today, forty-five years after the promulgation of *Sacrosanctum concilium*, we have barely scratched the surface as to what the

Council asked of the Church in the renewal of its worship. At this point in our history we are now able to look back over the post-Conciliar liturgical implementation with mature eyes to evaluate and discern what was done well and what was not done well. As mentioned earlier, few liturgical scholars today would argue that the 1973 *Sacramentary* was an adequate rendering in English of the Latin *editio typica* of the *Roman Missal*. But we must also remember that the *English Missal* was produced in haste in a record four years, and that those involved with the process did they best they could given the constraints of time and resources.

Having said that, however, as we reflect upon the liturgical renewal in the years since Vatican II we have a tremendous amount for which to be grateful. The Council's desire for full, active, and conscious participation has been realized in much of the Church throughout the English-speaking world, whether one considers parish life in the United Kingdom or Canada, the United States, or Australia. This is especially evident in the growth within lay ecclesial ministry and liturgical leadership. A concomitant growth has also been registered in liturgical formation – both for laity as well as clergy. Today, the Church of the twenty-first century recognizes more clearly that the handing on of the Church's tradition through its worship necessarily involves more than the clergy. It is a partnership shared between women and men, involving a complementary rather than competing exercise of ministry within the liturgical assembly as within the Church itself. Baptism not ordination appropriately becomes the common denominator in this equation and thus, at least ideally, the implications for ecumenical liturgical cooperation are obvious. This is not to deny the hierarchical structure of the Church nor to imply that the Church is a democracy; it is not. But, rather, to affirm the fundamental truth that each member of the Church is called to play an important role in Christ's mission under the leadership of the bishops, and this is especially evident in the diversity of ministries exercised within the liturgical assembly.

Like other Christian churches, the Roman Catholic Church has made great strides in recovering the intrinsic relationship between liturgy and life – worship that flows into social outreach of the poor and disenfranchised. Questions raised by the social sciences – new insights drawn from cultural studies have called our attention to the diverse dynamics at play when we gather for Christian worship, and the importance of worship that is contextualized according to the needs and parameters of the given celebrating community. Back in the 1970s some Roman Catholic liturgists in the United States called for an 'American Liturgy' that would reflect the genius of the North American cultural experience. But today Americans would need to ask themselves 'which America?' since we are much more conscious than we were thirty or forty years ago of our multiracial, multicultural, diverse identity, and the effects of globalization on our worship. The same, of course, is true in London or Glasgow, Sydney or Vancouver. And as *Sacrosanctum concilium* reminds us, attention to issues of cultural adaptation must always be given with respect to maintaining the 'substantial unity of the Roman Rite.' In 1988 when the Holy See approved the adapted form of the Roman Rite for the dioceses of Zaire (now the Democratic Republic of Congo), that ritual was entitled 'The Roman Rite for the Dioceses of Zaire' rather than the 'Zairean Rite,' faithful to the principle of the Roman Rite's substantial unity while allowing for some significant adaptation.

Today, however, tensions remain within the Church precisely around what is actually meant by the 'substantial unity of the Roman Rite' and just how much room there is for its contextualization or 'liturgical creativity.' Conservative scholars lament the loss of the transcendent within post-Conciliar Catholic worship, often presuming that proponents of the Conciliar reforms are content with the current state of affairs. They are not. While there is much to be commended in the post-Conciliar implementation of the liturgical reforms, there is also a significant level of reform that has not yet been introduced – in the area of liturgical catechesis and formation, for example. And much has to do with how to redress the balance between transcendence and immanence; recovering a sense of mystery and the sacred; the custody of words with greater attention to silence and the non-verbal. Interestingly, by and large our Anglican counterparts have done a far better job at this than Roman Catholics – maintaining a sense of dignity and reverence within liturgical celebrations; greater attention to mystery and the numinous without losing the participative dimension of worship so characteristic of what was desired by the Second Vatican Council. Forty-five years on, we must state it squarely: attention to the transcendent within worship and the Conciliar principle of 'full, active, and conscious liturgical participation' are not mutually exclusive. Indeed, greater attention to recovering a sense of mystery within worship might actually serve as a bridge to the constituency mentioned in the previous section that has remained critical of the *'novus ordo.'*[25]

What I have just stated is hugely important if we are to find a way forward in our liturgical discussions within the Roman Catholic Church – if we are to move away from the so-called 'liturgy wars' (Google listed more than 300,000 entries under that heading when I last checked), in favor of the ongoing renewal of the Church's worship – the 'true and indispensable source for the Christian life' as Pius X reminded us. In other words, it is a well-kept secret that liturgical scholars of different stripes are essentially on the same page when it comes to critiquing worship that has become overly verbose to the point of banality, lacking in silence and attention to the Church's rich symbolic system, and where the one presiding has become too central to the liturgical action. These same liturgical scholars would also agree in their critique of presiders who take liberties with improvising on liturgical texts like the Introductory Rite (e.g., 'Good morning everyone. I'm Father Bill and I'm your celebrant today!') or the Eucharistic Prayer; or in not observing the rubrics without even understanding why such rubrical directives were designed in the first place (e.g., inviting everyone to pray the 'Prayer for Peace' before the Breaking of Bread ('Lord Jesus Christ, you said to your apostles ...')).

I might also make reference to the ongoing crisis in liturgical music in many parts of the world. At a recent Sunday Mass during Lent in a cathedral church in central Italy – the principal Mass of the day – the opening song was entitled: *'Scusa Signore.'* ('Excuse me, Lord'), and the Lord's Prayer, also accompanied on guitar, was sung to the tune of Simon and Garfunkel's 'Sound of Silence.' My point here is that there is actually more consensus on post-Conciliar liturgical problems than meets the eye between centrist and conservative liturgical scholars, and even with ideological or reactionary liturgical critics. The capacity for self-criticism is a sign of health, and within the Church we should not presume that our liturgical life is not in need of ongoing evaluation and correction that will contribute to its eventual growth.

Conclusion

Ironically, the liturgy and especially the Eucharist – source of our unity – has become the source of our disunity. And such division within the Church, of course, is read as a scandal to those outside of it. If our own corporate witness as Roman Catholics is to have any merit at all beyond the parameters of our own Church, then we must make it our aim to work for the unity of the Church – our own, first, and then the wider unity of Christ's Church beyond Roman Catholicism. So it is time to move from the negative attacks on both sides of the issue – especially evident in the blogosphere – attacks which ultimately wound the body of Christ – and seek bridges to reconciliation so that the liturgical life within Christ's Church might once again become the source of unity it is intended to be. Of course, this unity is a divine rather than human construct. Only God can bring it about, but we can give ourselves over to it more intentionally if we choose to, and the time has come to do so.

Much of the consternation around the liturgical reforms has been regarding liturgical language – Latin or the vernacular – and around the translation of liturgical texts. In several years time the Church will offer us a new English translation of the *Roman Missal*. While much of the criticism of the earlier drafts was not without merit, it must also be acknowledged that the revised texts are a significant improvement over earlier editions and a number of them continue to be refined in various drafts. Forty-five years after the promulgation of *Sacrosanctum concilium* the

Church offers us a fresh opportunity for liturgical formation and catechesis which we were not afforded in the years immediately after the Second Vatican Council. I am speaking here not only about catechesis on the new *Missal* and liturgical translations but on the Conciliar liturgy itself – its ecclesiological and missiological dimension – and what our liturgical participation actually demands of us if we take it seriously. This will be further discussed in the fourth and fifth chapters. Before approaching that task, however, it is important to offer an explanation of how our process of translating liturgical texts grew and evolved since Vatican II, in order to better understand how we arrived at the present. Thus, in the following chapter, we shall consider the evolution of post-Conciliar liturgical translation.

Notes

1   See Keith F. Pecklers, 'The Jansenist Critique and the Liturgical Reforms of the Seventeenth and Eighteenth Centuries,' in *Ecclesia Orans* (2003/3), 325–338.

2   Olivier Rousseau, O.S.B., *The Progress of the Liturgy* (Westminster, Maryland: The Newman Press, 1951), 24.

3   *Motu Proprio of Pius X 'Tra le sollecitudini'* (22 November 1903), in *Acta Sanctae Sedis* 36:28 (1904), 331.

4   See for example, Alcuin Reid, *The Organic Development of the Liturgy* (Farnborough: Saint Michael's Abbey Press, 2004).

5   Nathan Mitchell, 'The Council's Call: On the Fortieth Anniversary of *Sacrosanctum Concilium* in *America* (19–26 January 2004), 9.

6   John O'Malley, 'Reform, Historical Consciousness and Vatican II's Aggiornamento,' *Theological Studies* 32 (1971), 573.

7   Anscar J. Chupungco, '*Sacrosanctum concilium:* Its Vision and Achievements,' in *Ecclesia Orans* XIII (1996/3), 498.

8   *Sacrosanctum concilium* 34.

9   Xavier Rynne, *Vatican Council II* (Maryknoll, New York: Orbis, 1999), 72.

10   Article 53.

11   Article 7.

12   Chupungco, 500. See Article 50 on the revision of the Order of Mass.

13   Article 37.

14   Article 40.
15   Article 22.
16   Article 41; Chupungco, 507–508.
17   Archbishop Piero Marini, *A Challenging Reform: Realizing the Vision of the Liturgical Renewal,* Mark R. Francis, C.S.V., John R. Page, Keith F. Pecklers, S.J., eds. (Collegeville: The Liturgical Press, 2007).
18   'Memorandum by the Liturgical Commission of the French Episcopate,' 7th February 1964, in Archbishop Piero Marini, *A Challenging Reform, Realizing the Vision of the Liturgical Renbewal,* Mark R. Francis, C.S.V., John R. Page, Keith F. Pecklers, S.J., eds. (Collegeville: The Liturgical Press, 2007), 168–170.
19   Marini, 12.
20   Marini Interview with Allen, 5–6.
21   Klaus Gamber, *The Modern Rite: Collected Essays on the Reform of the Liturgy* (Farnborough: St. Michael's Abbey Press, 2002), 7.
22   For an excellent analysis of *Summorum Pontificum,* see John F. Baldovin, 'Reflections on Summorum Pontificum,' in *Worship* 83/2 (March 2009), 98–112.
23   See Nicola Bux, *La Riforma di Benedetto XVI: La Liturgia tra Innovazione e Tradizione* (Casale Monferrato: Piemme, 2008).
24   Keith F. Pecklers, *The Unread Vision: The Liturgical Movement in the United States of America 1926–1955* (Collegeville: The Liturgical Press, 1998).
25   See John F. Baldovin, *Reforming the Liturgy: A Response to the Critics* (Collegeville: The Liturgical Press/Pueblo, 2008).

The Process of Liturgical Translation

3

Introduction

As we consider the Conciliar liturgical reforms of these past forty-five years and as we await the new English translation of the *Roman Missal*, a consideration of the post-Conciliar process of liturgical translation in the English-speaking world will help to frame our discussion in its proper historical context, and to explain the rationale for the new translations in the first place. For while there have been many reports about the new translations, for example about the fact that we will now be returning to the response 'And with your spirit' to the priest's 'The Lord be with you,' the rationale for such a linguistic shift has not always been articulated as clearly. Of course, had the English-language world originally translated the Latin original in such a manner immediately after the Council as was the case in most other language groups, we would not be in the position we are in today. Having become accustomed to saying 'and also with you' for the past forty years, the challenge is all the greater since the lay faithful understandably feel that something is being taken from them. Even more to the point, many read a conservative agenda into such a shift. The reality, however, is much more complicated, and that is what we wish to consider in this third chapter: the evolution of liturgical translation in the years since the Council – its process and the principles on which it is based.

Before we proceed, it is important briefly to consider how the subject of the vernacular was presented and discussed at the Second Vatican Council itself. We will then consider the foundation and work of the International Commission on English in the Liturgy (ICEL) charged with the task of translating liturgical books from the Latin typical edition (*editio typica*) into

English and how the documents *Comme le prevoit* (1969) and *Liturgiam authenticam* (2001) – both dealing with the process of liturgical translation – have shaped and guided its work.

The Vernacular Issue at the Second Vatican Council

One of the greatest gifts to vernacular promotion during the Ecumenical Council came on Sunday 4 November 1962 in the Vatican Basilica, at a Mass commemorating the fourth anniversary of John XXIII's coronation. The principal celebrant was the then Archbishop of Milan and future Pope Paul VI, Cardinal Montini. The occasion was already unusual in that it was one of the few times over the centuries in which the Ambrosian Rite of Milan had been celebrated in Saint Peter's. But it was even more distinctive in the language used as John XXIII addressed the gathered assembly at the end of the Mass. After the Pope praised Latin as the language 'in which the prelates of the universal Church communicate with the center of Catholicism,' he then spoke in Italian for the rest of his talk since it was better understood by those present – bishops included. The Pope concluded his remarks:

> It is perfectly natural that new times and new circumstances should suggest different forms and methods for transmitting externally the one and same doctrine, and of clothing it in a new dress. Yet the living substance is always the purity of the evangelical and apostolic truth, in perfect conformity with the teaching of holy Church, who often applies to herself the maxim, 'Only one art, but a thousand forms.'[1]

With the desire to recover 'full, conscious, and active participation in the liturgy,' the Council once again took up discussion on the vernacular question that had first been introduced at the Council of Trent four centuries prior, arguing in favor of the employment of local languages on the grounds of intelligibility.[2] Not surprisingly, it proved to be one of the most hotly debated topics at Vatican II. There were some bishops present at the

Council who, reiterating the position at the Council of Trent in light of the Reformation, contended that Latin, even if it was not understood by most, gave Catholics a special identity. Shifting to local languages, they argued, would be tantamount to abandoning Catholic orthodoxy. Cardinal Francis Spellman of New York was one such bishop. Speaking on the matter during one Council session, he cautioned against 'an exaggerated historicism and a zeal for novelties.' He suggested that 'confusion, astonishment, and injury' could ensue when the faithful 'see the unchangeable Church changing her rites.' That said, however, the Cardinal was not exactly the best Latinist himself. During Council sessions, it became so painful when Spellman stood up to address his colleagues in Latin that Vatican staff members were assigned to another microphone with the task of translating the Cardinal's Latin into correct Latin so that he could be understood. So the Cardinal proposed a vernacular compromise: he would accept the vernacular for praying the Breviary (Divine Office) since he himself had difficulty in grasping what he was praying; but the celebration of Mass should remain in Latin.[3] That caused one Italian archbishop to exclaim: '*Ah questi americani!* Now they want the priest to pray in English, and the people to pray in Latin!'[4]

Everyone breathed a great sigh of relief when the 84-year-old Patriarch of Antioch, His Beatitude Maximos IV Saigh addressed the bishops in French, arguing that he was Catholic but not Roman Catholic, and Latin was not the language of his liturgical tradition. He argued that the text should be altered to state clearly that Latin 'is the original and official language of the Roman Rite.' Moreover, in the tradition of the Eastern Rites and consistent with what the French Liturgical Commission wrote in their 1964 memorandum quoted in the last chapter, episcopal conferences should decide on whatever vernacular they deemed to be appropriate for their regions, always subject to the approval of the Holy See. His addressed the issue squarely in his intervention:

The almost absolute value assigned to Latin in the liturgy, in teaching, and in the administration of the Latin church strikes us from the Eastern church as strange. Christ after all spoke the language of his contemporaries ... [In the East] there has never been a problem about the proper liturgical language. All languages are liturgical, as the Psalmist says, 'Praise the Lord, all ye people.' ... The Latin language is dead. But the church is living, and its language, the vehicle of the grace of the Holy Spirit, must also be living because it is intended for us human beings not for angels.

On the same day as Patriarch Maximos's intervention, Pope John XIII wrote in his diary that the subject of Latin divided the Second Vatican Council into those who had never left their own country 'or Italy' and those who had a more international vision of the Church because of the experience of living in a country and culture which was not their own.[5] Undoubtedly, the shift toward vernacular worship represented one of the most profound developments that came out of the Council. And, in fact, it received no small amount of attention in the secular press – everything from the *New York Times* and *Wall Street Journal* to *Sports Illustrated* and *Time*.

One of the most memorable pro-vernacular statements from outside the Council came from Professor A.H. Armstrong in the form of an open letter sent to the bishops of England, Wales, and Scotland in September, 1963. While he had intended it to be a letter of gratitude to the bishops for their support of the vernacular at the Council's First Session, it reads more like a treatise or bold affirmation in favor of the subject. The bishops were particularly taken by Armstrong's text since he was the Gladstone Professor of Greek at the University of Liverpool, which made his pro-vernacular testimony all the more intriguing. He wrote:

The decision of the Council that the vernacular is in principle admissible to the Liturgy is most welcome both for historical and pastoral reasons, and should be implemented, by introducing as much vernacular into the Liturgy as quickly as possible, in the English-speaking world ... The claim that Latin is in any peculiar and exclusive sense 'the language of the Church' is not historically well founded (and is intensely irritating to Eastern Christians in and out of communion with Rome, as it ignores their own immemorial traditions). Latin is not the original language of a single book of inspired Scripture. It was not used by Our Lord, Our Lady or any of the Apostles. It was not the language of SS Peter and Paul, or of the Roman Church until the third or fourth centuries AD when it was substituted for Greek because it was the current vernacular. If we really want to be faithful to the tradition of the Apostles and martyrs of Rome, we who use the Roman Rite should translate the Liturgy as quickly as possible in our several vernaculars. No saint mentioned in our Canon would have thought otherwise.[6]

The Foundation of the International Commission on English in the Liturgy (ICEL) and Joint Commissions for Liturgical Translation

Only weeks before the promulgation of *Sacrosanctum concilium*, a meeting of more than a dozen bishops representing various English-speaking countries was held on 17 October 1963 at the Venerable English College in Rome to discuss plans for 'a liturgical English language vernacular text to be used in the Catholic Mass and Sacraments.'[7] The meeting was chaired by Francis Grimshaw, the Archbishop of Birmingham. Australia was well represented by Guilford Young of Hobart who was one of the strongest voices for the renewal of Catholic worship among all the English-speaking bishops gathered at Vatican II. Immediately, those bishops gathered at the English College recognized the need to include biblical scholars, musicologists, and linguistic scholars for the credibility of the translations in order to ensure an English text true to the needs of public worship, as well as musical and literary requirements. The goal was to create liturgical texts that would win wide acceptance across the English-speaking world.

With the approval of the Council's Liturgy Constitution on 4 December 1963 and the extraordinary attention given to the introduction of local languages into Catholic worship, it was not surprising that a survey of journalists voted 'English in the Liturgy' the top religious story of 1964. On 25 January 1964, the fifth anniversary of John XXIII's convocation of the Council, Pope Paul VI promulgated the *Motu proprio Sacram liturgiam* – a restrictive document allowing only limited use of what the Council had promised, desiring to facilitate a gradual implementation rather than allowing for too much too soon. One of the greatest criticisms of the document came from episcopal conferences which resented the fact that they were not allowed to approve the translation of liturgical texts at the local level as the Council had proposed, but would rather need to submit their texts to the Holy See for the *recognitio* or official Vatican approval. It is interesting to note that it was not the English-speaking episcopal conferences that were critical of the *Motu proprio*, but rather the Bishops' Conferences of Austria, Germany, Italy, Spain, and especially France, as has already been seen.

The International *Consilium* moved forward with its task of implementing the liturgical reforms, nonetheless, and led the way in the process of reception of the new vernacular texts. On 16 October 1964, the President of the *Consilium* Cardinal Giacomo Lercaro wrote to all the presidents of episcopal conferences were there was a language shared between several different countries: Dutch, English, French, German, Italian, and Spanish. In that letter he expressed the *Consilium*'s desire to maintain a uniformity of language where possible avoiding unnecessary duplication of liturgical texts. Throughout the year of 1964 concrete form was given to the first hopes and proposals of liturgical translation. This led to the formal establishment of international liturgical commissions. It is within such a context that ten English-speaking conferences of bishops gave their formal mandate to the International Commission on English in the Liturgy.

There was essentially little problem within the English and French language groups, although the bishops of England and Wales initially wanted to go in their own direction by producing distinct translations. They soon abandoned that plan, however, in favor of joining the other English-speaking episcopal conferences. Problems were more pronounced in those conferences using Dutch: the Netherlands and the Flemish region of Belgium. Initially, the Dutch Conference resisted the idea of translating from the Latin typical edition, preferring to create original liturgical texts instead. They eventually conceded.

There were also problems among the Spanish-speaking conferences. Argentina, for example, continued to translate and publish pre-Conciliar liturgical texts on its own for a period of time. In Latin America, in general, liturgical scholars and translators were in short supply, so those episcopal conferences were forced to accept liturgical translations that had been produced in Spain. For obvious historic reasons, this was an unwelcome solution. Aside from political reasons for not welcoming imported texts from Spain, Spanish usage in Latin America had distinct differences from Castillian spoken in Spain. For example, there were the differences in translating: '*Dominus vobiscum*' was 'vosotros' in Spain, 'ustedes' in the majority of Latin American countries. Similar problems were registered in the episcopal conferences of Portugal and Brasil as they endeavored to find common ground in their liturgical use of Portugese.[8]

Recognizing the complexity and tensions regarding the translation process, the *Consilium* hosted an international meeting in Rome from 9 to 13 November 1965. It gathered an impressive group of 249 bishops, translators, liturgical scholars, and composers who hailed from sixty-nine countries and five continents.[9] On 10 November Pope Paul VI addressed the group in the Sala Clementina. Translations into the vernacular, he told them, 'have become part of the rites themselves; they have become the voice of the Church gathered in prayer. They now serve a different purpose,' he said, 'for they are no longer merely aids to understanding for those untrained in Latin.' That time had passed.[10] Put differently, we could say today that each vernacular language has its own inherent genius – English included – and is capable and indeed worthy of worshiping almighty God.

Comme le prévoit

With the work of the *Consilium* moving forward, the year 1969 brought the publication of the Instruction *Comme le prévoit* on the norms for translation of liturgical texts. In many respects, the document can be seen as an elaboration of what Paul VI had stated in his November 1965 address to translators. Another such meeting was held in 1967, at which representatives of the major language groups offered a draft document which included subsequent reflections on the 1965 meeting. That led to a Latin version of a draft text on liturgical translation prepared in early 1968 which was then presented to a general meeting of the *Consilium* in October of that year. As the original text was written in French it kept its French title. The *Consilium* had produced a translation in six languages and Pope Paul VI reviewed an Italian version of the text. As the text was produced in haste, the Pope's forty-seven corrections in eleven pages had as much to do with grammatical problems and syntax as they did with liturgical matters related to the Instruction. He completed his review and approved the text on 29 December 1968, and it was officially promulgated one month later on 25 January 1969 – exactly ten years to the day after the Second Vatican Council had been announced.[11]

By and large, *Comme le prévoit* was a hopeful and forward-looking document that envisaged three stages for the gradual implementation of vernacular worship: a preliminary translation of the typical edition of liturgical books; a subsequent revision based on evaluation and pastoral experience in the reception of the given texts; and new liturgical compositions based on number 40 of *Sacrosanctum concilium* which might better respond to the particular cultural contexts and pastoral exigencies of geographical regions and countries. The operative translation principle running throughout that Instruction was that of 'dynamic equivalence,' in which texts were to be translated dynamically so that they were intelligible and came alive appropriately within the particular vernacular in question. At number 7, for example, we read that translations 'must be faithful to the art of communication in all its aspects.' Number

6 is even more direct: 'A faithful translation, therefore, cannot be judged on the basis of individual words: the total context of the specific act of communication must be kept in mind, as well as the literary form proper to the respective language.'

Number 13 argued that terms to address God – *quaesumus*; *dignare*; *clementissime*; *maiestas*; etc. – had a particular role within the Byzantine or Roman court. We need to ask ourselves if there are not better, more appropriate, terms in which to address God. At the same time, Number 15 warns against the use of banal, common language. Number 20 affirms that the prayer of the Church is always a prayer of this or that particular Church at a given moment in its history, thus it is not enough to simply translate a term verbatim. Rather, the prayer needs to in some way be incarnated, taking on the flesh and blood of the community that gathers for worship. At the end of the day, *Comme le prévoit* was a consultative document that could trace its origins back to that 1965 meeting of several hundred translators from every corner of the globe. Its revisions made by the *Consilium* and indeed, by the Pope himself, were made in a collegial manner typical of the Council itself – in concert with episcopal conferences around the world who would ultimately be responsible for implementing the Instruction on liturgical translation.

The Work of ICEL in the 1970s through the 1990s

By 1973 ICEL had completed its work on the first edition of the *Sacramentary* in English and this was approved by the now eleven-member episcopal conferences in 1974–1975. As work on the *Sacramentary* neared completion, the Advisory Commitee of ICEL recommended to ICEL's Episcopal Board that the *Sacramentary* be introduced for a limited period *Ad experimentum* – perhaps for a period of five years. But the bishops thought that there had been enough provisional texts and it would not be pastorally prudent to extend this for an additional period. So the Sacramentary was approved in 1975.

ICEL moved into a second stage of revision and with the publication of the second edition of the *Roman Missal* in Latin, the first consultation on the revision of the *Sacramentary* was held on 4 October 1982 and continued through 1983. Those intimately involved in the project recognized the many deficiencies of the 1973 *Sacramentary*. It was clear, for example, that the presidential prayers would need total recasting rather than simply minor revisions and that work began substantially in 1984. Already in the 1982–1983 consultations a clear desire was surfacing for alternative opening prayers that would correspond to the three-year lectionary. In fact, such texts began appearing in the sacramentaries of other language groups, most notably in the Italian revised *Messale Romano* of 1982.

But unlike the other language groups, the English-speaking world would have a far more difficult time in agreeing on proposed liturgical texts within the various episcopal conferences, but even more so in the episcopal conferences' relationship to the Congregation for Divine Worship and the Discipline of the Sacraments. While it is not easy to ascertain exactly what went wrong in the process, there was a fundamental communication problem at play between the Congregation and ICEL's Episcopal Board, not to mention within the bishops' conferences themselves. And this, unfortunately, led to certain impressions within the Congregation that ICEL, for example, was being controlled by feminists, given the significant attention paid to inclusive language – an issue which had not yet reached the Mediterranean world although that is no longer the case. ICEL came to be seen as a progressive body which needed to be watched carefully. In the practical order, this meant that as Italian, French, German, Portugese, Spanish, and other language groups saw the revisions of their own Missals approved and implemented throughout the 1980s, with the inclusion of alternative opening prayers and eventually the so-called 'Swiss Synod Eucharistic Prayers' – promulgated as the Latin typical edition in 1991 with the title 'Eucharistic Prayers for Various Needs and Occasions' – the English-speaking world held steady with its 1973 *Sacramentary*, despite ICEL's continued efforts through the 1980s and 1990s.

Many of the themes found in *Comme le prévoit* were further developed almost thirty years later in an article by Robert Taft entitled 'Translating Liturgically.' He writes: 'One's first interpretation of a passage is always the translation, and to pretend that a translation is not in a very real sense an *interpretation* of the original is to be completely ignorant of both the nature of language and the nature of translating.'[12] He then proceeds to argue that translation for public worship necessitates a distinct set of issues that need to be considered if the translation is to be effective:

> Liturgical English is not the English of a scholarly translation or a detective story. It is not the English of narrative dialogue, but also not the English of Hopkins'or Eliot's poetry. And I might add, if we are doing the translation for people of today, and doing it, presumably, so that they will understand it, since the only reason we are doing it is that they no longer understand Greek or Old Slavonic, then it should be in the English of today and not of the sixteenth century.[13]

Taft offers a helpful principle regarding liturgical translation from typical editions: 'The aim of a good translation is to be faithful to two languages, the donor and the recipient. But in case of conflict, the recipient language takes precedence, all other things being equal.'[14]

One bishop who spoke out forcefully during the 1990s in favor of a greater role for episcopal conferences in decision making on matters liturgical was the late Scottish Cardinal Thomas Winning, Archbishop of Glasgow. The Cardinal who was known to be quite conservative in most other areas, criticized the Congregation for Divine Worship's excessive intervention in the work of ICEL, arguing that doing so was an attack on the fundamental principles of collegiality: if diocesan bishops and bishops' conferences have approved liturgical translations as doctrinally sound, properly translated, and proclaimable, it was not the place of the Congregation to deem otherwise. The Korean and Japanese Episcopal Conferences weighed in on the discussion during the Asian Synod, arguing that their situation is further complicated by the fact that no one in the Congregation is proficient in those Asian languages. or *English*?

Ever the eternal optimist and still believing that the ICEL's revised *Sacramentary* would see the light of day, I published *Liturgy for the New Millennium: A Commentary on the Revised Sacramentary* in the year 2000 along with Mark R. Francis, C.S.V., then Professor of Liturgical Inculturation at the Catholic Theological Union in Chicago. While the book was ostensibly a *festschrift* for our doctoral mentor at the Pontifical Liturgical Institute, Anscar Chupungco – the Filipino Benedictine who is the godfather of liturgical inculturation – it was intended to help clergy and lay pastoral leaders to understand various changes in the new *Sacramentary*. One such change was to be the movement of the greeting of peace from its current position to after the General Intercessions as a bridge between the Word and Eucharist. We had hoped that our book would assist the implementation and reception of the revised liturgical text much like this book in relation to the third edition of the *Roman Missal*. The conservative Catholic lobbyist Helen Hull Hitchcock immediately wrote a negative review of the book entitled 'Jumping the Gun,' which she published in the Latin Mass journal *Adoremus*. And of course, she was right! The English-language translation of the second edition of the *Roman Missal* never did see the light of day and with the publication of *Liturgiam authenticam (LA)* in 2001 and then the third Latin typical edition of the *Roman Missal* since the Council – ICEL's efforts of almost twenty years became a moot point.

Now, it is no secret that for the past thirty years or so, opposition to the *novus ordo* has intensified, and much of this animosity has focused largely on the translation process. 'Translation wars' are nothing new, of course, but rather are as old as the Church itself. It would be enough to consider the numerous revisions of the Greek translation of the Hebrew Bible, the *Septuagint*. And even before Saint Jerome finished his work on the Vulgate, he came under strong attack from conservative critics.[15] Jerome wrote in response: 'If I translate word by word, it sounds absurd; if I am forced to change something in the word of style, I seem to have stopped being a translator.' In fact, Jerome wisely employed the Latin that was commonly spoken by the *vulgus* – the crowd – thus the name *vulgate* – and not the more rarified or elegant Latin of Cicero or Julius Caesar. This was precisely so that the people would be able to understand the richness found within the Sacred Scriptures. So these post-Conciliar tensions in the realm of liturgical translation are part of the Church's ongoing evolution. Commenting on Jerome's response to his critics, Anscar Chupungco wrote:

> With these words St. Jerome articulated the experience of every conscientious translator. Word-by-word translation often does not make sense, but a change in the meaning of the word betrays the message. The translation of liturgical texts is perhaps the most delicate and complex matter arising from the Church's decision to shift from Latin to the vernacular languages.[16]

Lest we think that we in the Roman Catholic Church are the only ones suffering with translation issues, it should also be mentioned that the situation in the Christian East has had to endure its own translation tensions, even despite the positive reading of that subject rendered by Maximos IV at Vatican II. In many Eastern Christian liturgies an older form of the vernacular is used. So in the Greek Orthodox tradition, for example, ancient and Byzantine Greek texts are employed while Old Slavonic is the 'vernacular' language used within Russian Orthodox worship. Thus, while they are related to the mother tongues of most worshipers in those traditions, a good number of psalm texts, readings from the Pauline corpus, and numerous hymns and other liturgical texts are almost completely unintelligible to them. And as language continues to evolve, several Greek words used in the Gospels have acquired a different meaning over the centuries. For example, the Greek word *malakia* meaning 'weakness' or 'sickness' now means 'masturbation' or 'dirty trick' in modern-day Greek. Thus, many priests replace the word with another, such as *astheneia*, when preaching or in other liturgical contexts, but they are reluctant to do so when reading the Gospels. Not surprisingly, one finds more than a few congregants smiling at that point as Jesus cures the 'masturbation' or 'dirty trick' of those he was healing!

As an effort to deal with the issue of intelligibility within liturgical texts, several Slavic churches including the Russian Orthodox Church now read the scriptural readings in modern Russian just before Communion, having read them first in Old Slavonic during the Liturgy of the Word.[17] By way of contrast, Romanian, Serbian, and Georgian Orthodox Churches normally use modern day vernacular in their own liturgical prayer.

Liturgiam authenticam: A New Era in Liturgical Translation

When *Liturgiam authenticam (LA)* was issued in 2001 it introduced a new set of directives for liturgical translation which placed new restrictions on the process, insisting on a more faithful and doctrinally sound translation at all cost. It also abrogated the 1969 Instruction *Comme le prévoit*, insisting that all subsequent translations would need to follow the strict translation principles stated in the new Instruction. Soon after its publication, one prominent European cardinal expressed his surprise at the new document and asked me where it had come from. Even though he is a Member of the Congregation for Divine Worship and the Discipline of the Sacraments, he was unaware that the document was in preparation and only learned of it when he read about it in the press. Indeed, unlike the earlier Instruction *Comme le prévoit*, the 2001 Instruction was not produced in a consultative and collegial manner, but rather produced in haste and in secret. This, unfortunately, has hurt the document's credibility, especially in the realm of its reception.

By way of background, there are several important points worth mentioning in order better to understand the rationale for the publication of *Liturgiam authenticam* in the first place. It needs to be said from the outset that the authors of *LA* are convinced of the fact that the syntax of the Latin actually contains doctrine. Thus, the use of antithesis, for example, or words of supplication like *quaesumus* is not just convention, but contains profound theological truths and needs to be replicated in English. Second, it is commonly known that very few Asian translations of liturgical books are made from the Latin *editio typica* but rather from English. Hence the demand of the Congregation for Divine Worship for literal texts also stems from a concern for faithful translation in Chinese and Japanese, Korean and Thai, as well as other Asian languages. Third, the Congregation was concerned about the emergence of original texts which have no antecedents in liturgical books of the Roman Rite, such as is found in the current Italian *Missal*, which offers Collect prayers corresponding to the three-year cycle of the Roman Lectionary. Those same Collect prayers are also found in ICEL's proposed second edition of the *Roman Missal*. *LA* would now curtail original texts because of new principles established in the document.

Liturgiam authenticam did more than establish new directives for liturgical translation, however. New burdens were placed upon the translation process and, indeed, upon translators themselves, and a new era of vernacular worship emerged. A new ICEL team was put in place, and translators were now required to seek the *Nihil obstat* before collaborating as liturgical translators. While *Liturgiam authenticam* was addressed primarily to ICEL and the English-speaking world, it had obvious implications for other language groups as well. Indeed, from my travels around the world, to the best of my knowledge the only language group that is *not* struggling with their translations is that of the young Church in Mongolia – only seventeen years old. That Church recently received approval for its Lectionary in Mongol in a record few months!

A word about *Liturgiam authenticam*'s content is in order. Entitled 'The Fifth Instruction for the Right Implementation of the Constitution on the Sacred Liturgy of the Second Vatican Council,' *LA* acknowledges the positive results of the Conciliar liturgical renewal. Nonetheless,

> the greatest prudence and attention is required in the preparation of liturgical books marked by sound doctrine,

which are exact in wording, free from ideological influence, and otherwise endowed with those qualities by which the sacred mysteries of salvation and the indefectible faith of the Church are efficaciously transmitted by means of human language to prayer.[18]   *Agreed*

Liturgical texts are also to avoid any 'psychologizing tendency' within the translation.[19] These references to 'ideological influence' and a 'psychologizing tendency' are two of the clearest indications that the document is directed to the English-speaking world, especially regarding the issue of inclusive language, where that linguistic group led the way. From various conversations with cardinals and bishops in Rome, and especially in discussions with liturgical colleagues in Rome and elsewhere, most point to the document's inconsistencies and contradictions. This is especially clear, for example, when we read the text side by side with the Liturgy Constitution *Sacrosanctum concilium*. Nathan Mitchell of the University of Notre Dame in the United States has made such a comparison in his regular column in *Worship* entitled 'The Amen Corner.'

I offer just one example: *Sacrosanctum concilium* 21 states: 'In this restoration [of the liturgy] both texts and rites should be drawn up so as to express more clearly the holy things which they signify. The Christian people, as far as possible, should be able to understand them with ease and take part in them fully, actively, and as a community.' And again, 'The rites should be distinguished by a noble simplicity. They should be short, clear, and free of useless repetitions. They should be within the people's power of comprehension, and normally should not require much explanation.'[20] Yet, in *Liturgiam authenticam* we read: 'It should be borne in mind that a literal translation of terms which may initially sound odd in a vernacular language may for this very reason provoke inquisitiveness in the hearer and provide an occasion for catechesis.'[21] *Crap!*

Commenting on such a contradiction, Mitchell writes:

This suggests that – when preparing Lectionary translations – it is permissible (even desirable) to chose 'odd' vernacular expressions that will provoke 'inquisitiveness' and hence 'provide an occasion for catechesis.' How does *LA* 43 tally with *SC*'s insistence that texts and rites should be 'within the people's power of comprehension?' In fact, an earlier paragraph (27) of *LA* cautions translators to avoid 'expressions ... which hinder the comprehension because of their excessively unusual or awkward nature.'[22]

For his part, the former Prefect of the Congregation for Divine Worship and the Discipline of the Sacraments, Cardinal Francis Arinze, who was not involved in the preparation of *Liturgiam Authenticam*, has argued that 'intelligibility should not be pushed to mean that every word must be understood by everybody at once. Translators should not become iconoclasts who leave a path of destruction and damage in their wake. Not everything can be explained during the liturgy.'[23]

In his text, *Translating Tradition: A Chant Historian Reads 'Liturgiam authenticam.'* the conservative scholar Peter Jeffery notes further flaws in the text. *LA* 65 states that 'The Creed is to be translated according to the precise wording that the tradition of the Latin Church has bestowed upon it, including the use of the first person singular.' Thus, as we will see in Chapter 5, the new requirement in the revised *Ordo missae* will be to say 'I believe' (*Credo*) rather than 'We believe' (*Credimus*) that we have been saying since the Council. The document argues that this change is imperative so as to be consistent with the tradition of the Latin Church. The only problem is that this simply isn't true. The original texts of the 'Nicene Creed' published in Greek and Latin by the early ecumenical councils consistently began 'We believe.' In fact, even Pope Leo the Great cited the use of 'We believe' and we find the same in early Roman collections of Canon Law. And both before and after Vatican II, the Spanish or Mozarabic Rite used and continues to use 'We believe.'[24]

Many more contradictions within the document could be noted. There is an apparent belief evident in the text that vernacular languages can actually be fitted into Latin syntax – thus the problem in some of the Collect prayers which are composed in a single sentence to correspond to the Latin original as shall be discussed in the final chapter. But English, of course, like other vernacular languages, has its own genius, its own history, and its own syntax, which simply cannot be transliterated from Latin. There is also a certain confusion between archaic and sacral language. We are all in agreement that we need to recover appropriate sacral language as we long to worship God in 'spirit and truth.' And we are also in agreement that the 1973 *Sacramentary* left much to be desired in this regard. But this does not mean that we should employ archaic language such as the 'gibbet of the cross.' The argument in favor of 'gibbet' was that it was an English term used by St. John Fisher (+1535). But as Bishop Vincent Galeone of St. Augustine Florida argued in an article published in *America* Magazine, 'St. John Fisher also used the term "forsooth." Do we also wish to use "forsooth" rather than "indeed" for a more accurate rendering of the Latin *vere*?,' he asked. [25]

Liturgiam authenticam also presents fresh challenges for the issue of liturgical translation in the realm of ecumenism. In his Aidan Kavanagh lecture at Yale University in October 2006, Lutheran liturgical scholar Maxwell Johnson raised the serious ecumenical concerns and limits which that document now imposes, potentially impeding our future efforts at ecumenical liturgical cooperation. [26] Similar concerns have been voiced by Presbyterian liturgical pioneer Horace Allen[27] and Anglican Canon Donald Gray, President of the Alcuin Club.[28] Language, of course, is itself symbolic, and holding liturgical texts in common communicates something quite profound about what we believe regarding common baptism. In other words, even as we sadly remain divided around the altar of the Holy Eucharist, we need not be divided at the altar of God's Word – both the Word proclaimed and the texts we pray in common. Thus, our ecumenical partners find it lamentable that the Roman Catholic Church will soon have translations of the *Gloria, Credo, Sanctus* which no longer match those of other churches – lamentable especially since those other churches generously adopted Roman translations in the revisions of their own liturgical books. They argue that, forty-five years after the promulgation of *Sacrosanctum concilium,* it is difficult to see this as progress.

As a response to *Liturgiam authenticam* and further to monitor the liturgical translation process in the English-speaking world, the *Vox Clara* Commission was established in July 2002 to oversee the work of the International Commission on English in the Liturgy. ICEL revised its statutes in 2003 to comply with the requirements of *Liturgiam authenticam*, and the *Ratio translationis* followed in draft form in 2005 and was finally approved in 2007; it is meant to remain untouched for five years until 2012 when it may be evaluated again. The *Ratio translationis* notes that the goal of translation is to create a ' liturgical vernacular' which

> faithfully ... conveys the language and content of the prayers of the Roman Rite for public proclamation. The corresponding 'sacral' or 'liturgical' vernacular will reflect not only Catholic belief, but also the important ways in which the Roman Rite has expressed such belief over the centuries. Not unexpectedly, such a 'syntax-in-translation' will sometimes differ noticeably from ordinary speech in the same language.'[29]

Our new liturgical translations, then, are borne within such a context.

Conclusion

This brief historical sweep of the Conciliar reforms is instructive as we move toward consideration of the most recent General Instruction on the *Roman Missal* in the next chapter and the new English translation of the *Roman Missal* in Chapter 5. One can lament the loss of *Comme le prévoit* in favor of a more restrictive document on liturgical translation – a document which, as we have seen above, is not unproblematic. Some bishops and liturgical colleagues see the document and subsequent process of liturgical translation as impinging upon Conciliar principles of collegiality inherent within their episcopal leadership, while others express pastoral concerns about the limits which the new document places upon the translation process, resulting in the eventual problem of reception of the new text on the diocesan level.

As has already been mentioned, these problems and concerns are not limited to the English-speaking world. Colleagues working on the translation of the third edition of the *Missale Romanum* into French, German, Italian, and Spanish have recounted to me their own struggles to produce faithful vernacular translations that comply with the norms established by *Liturgiam authenticam*. Asian colleagues have an even greater challenge as they endeavor to translate the typical editions into Japanese, Korean, Mandarin Chinese, and numerous other languages that do not easily offer a composite or close equivalent to the Latin original.

That said, however, we must deal with the translation document we have been given, and do the best to render the best liturgical translations possible within the parameters established by *Liturgiam authenticam*. Translators are keenly aware of such challenges and doing the best that they can possibly do, in my opinion. Without being overly simplistic or naive about the problems that do exist and having expressed some of the reservations that bishops and liturgical scholars have regarding the new translations, it is now time to come together and move forward in hope. Moreover, proper liturgical formation and catechesis on the new *Missal* and its eventual implementation will need to be carefully orchestrated so that this is carried out effectively and not in haste. As we shall see in Chapter 5, while the new texts are significantly improved over earlier drafts, they are not perfect. Only God is perfect. We need to be honest and realistic as we approach the task of implementation, but we do need to get on with the task. Our next chapter will explore the contents of the revised *General Instruction of the Roman Missal* which will govern our process of implementing the new *Missal*.

Notes

1   Quoted in Xavier Rynne, *Vatican Council II* (Maryknoll, New York: Orbis Books, 1999), 71–72.
2   Art. 36. On the vernacular debate at the Council see Keith F. Pecklers, S.J., *Dynamic Equivalence: The Living Language of Christian Worship* (Collegeville: The Liturgical Press, 2003), 170–225.
3   Pecklers, 170–215.
4   Rynne, 73.
5   John W. O'Malley, *What Happened at Vatican II* (Cambridge, Mass.: The Belknap Press of Harvard University Press, 2008), 136.
6   Professor A.H. Armstrong, 'An Open Letter Addressed to the Most Reverend Archbishops and the Right Reverend Bishops of the Hierarchy of England and Wales and the Hierarchy of Scotland, 15 September 1963, quoted in Pecklers, 197–198.
7   Quoted in Pecklers, 204.
8   Annibale Bugnini, *The Reform of the Liturgy 1948–1975* (Collegeville: The Liturgical Press, 219–221), 233–235.
9   Bugnini, 219–221.
10 Bugnini, 221–222.
11 Bugnini, 236–237.
12 Robert F. Taft, S.J., 'Translating Liturgically,' in *Logos: A Journal of Eastern Christian Studies* 39/2–4 (1998), 157.
13 Ibid.
14 Taft, 159.
15 Nathan Mitchell, 'The Amen Corner: Croquet with Flamingoes,' *Worship* 77/5 (September, 2003).
16 Anscar J. Chupungco, 'The Translation of Liturgical Texts,' in *Handbook for Liturgical Studies: Introduction to the Liturgy*, ed. Anscar J. Chupungco (Collegeville: The Liturgical Press, 1997), I: 388.
17 Bert Groen, 'New Challenges for the Study of Eastern Christian Liturgy,' *Bollettino della Badia Greca di Grottaferrata* 4 (2007), 93–95.
18 *LA* 3.
19 *LA* 54.
20 *SC* 34.
21 *LA* 43.
22 Mitchell, 462.
23 Cardinal Francis Arinze, 'Language in the Roman Rite,' *Antiphon* 11/2 (2007), 11.
24 Peter Jeffery, *Translating Tradition: A Chant Historian Reads Liturgiam Authenticam* (Collegeville: The Liturgical Press, 2005), 18–19.

25   Victor Galeone, 'Expressing Holy Things: Why Liturgical Language Should Be Accurate, Faithful, and Clear,' in *America* (September 8, 2008), 15–18.

26   Maxwell E. Johnson, 'The Loss of a Common Language: The End of Ecumenical Liturgical Convergence?' *Studia Liturgica* 37/1 (2007), 55–72.

27   Horace T. Allen, Jr., 'Common Lectionary and Protestant Hymnody: Unity at the Table of the Word – Liturgical and Ecumenical Bookends,' in James F. Puglisi, ed., *Liturgical Renewal as a Way to Christian Unity* (Collegeville: The Liturgical Press/Pueblo, 2005), 61–69.

28   Donald Gray, 'The Birth of the Joint Liturgical Group and Its Contribution to the Concept of Ecumenical Liturgical Co-Operation,' *The Record: The Church Service Society* 41 (Winter 2005/6), 23–35.

29   *Ratio Translationis* 110.

The 2002 *General Instruction on the Roman Missal* 4

Introduction

The late American liturgical pioneer Robert Hovda (+1991) regularly read the article on choreography in the 'Arts and Leisure' section of the Sunday *New York Times* to see what he might learn about liturgical unity within the ritual action. The *General Instruction on the Roman Missal (GIRM)* offers us such a choreography – a guide or set of directions and principles for a proper celebration of the liturgy. Serving as a Preface to the *Roman Missal* it also articulates the Church's understanding of the Eucharistic celebration. As early as the sixteenth century the Church had become concerned about such choreography so that liturgical celebrations could be enacted with dignity and reverence and better facilitate the unity of the one Body of Christ exhibited in the unity within the liturgical action. Of course, Trent's excessive emphasis on rubrical correctness at all cost presented another host of problems and contributed to an overly scrupulous clergy, fearful of erring in pronouncing a liturgical text under pain of mortal sin. Vatican II redressed the balance as seen in Number 21 of the 2002 *Instruction*: 'The purpose of this Instruction is to offer general guidelines for arranging the Eucharistic celebration properly and to set forth the rules of ordering the individual forms of celebration.'

An examination of the *2002 General Instruction on the Roman Missal* provides us with an opportunity not only to look at what is new or what has changed from the earlier *Instruction*, but also to reflect on the underlying theological principles and reasons that lie behind the text itself. In other words, the 2002 *Instruction* offers us an opportunity to take stock of our post-Conciliar liturgical history forty-five years on. Just five years ago on the First Sunday of Advent 2004, we marked the fortieth anniversary of the first Masses celebrated in English. As we saw in Chapter 2, the years immediately after the close of Vatican II offered precious little time for careful planning on how best to implement the reforms. And even though the *General Instruction* was placed at the very beginning of the *Sacramentary* where it continues to be found, it has often been overlooked. This has led to uneven results in just how successfully the reforms have been implemented.

As we consider the context of 2002 *Instruction*, it is important that it be seen as a transitional text just as was the case in its earlier editions. The *General Instruction* has changed several times since it was first introduced in 1969; it includes cultural and regional specifications due to conferences of bishops; and it contains good principles in addition to very detailed directions. This is a far cry from the rigidity of the Tridentine Rite. In this chapter, I would like to consider the historical context for the *General Instruction;* the contemporary pastoral situation; and the opportunities which the new *Instruction* offers us in terms of liturgical catechesis and formation.

Foundations in the Council of Trent

As we saw in the first chapter, it was the great British historian Edmund Bishop who unearthed the nature and characteristics of the Roman Rite itself: 'simplicity, practicality ... , gravity and dignity, soberness and sense.' Despite the primacy of Rome and various attempts to have other rites suppressed, the Roman Rite was but one of numerous liturgical rites observed in the West until the Tridentine reforms, even as it held a certain primacy over the others. There were diocesan rites such as the Sarum Rite of the Diocese of Salisbury in England which was also used in a number of neighboring dioceses. There was the Ambrosian Rite of the Archdiocese of Milan in northern Italy which contained some liturgical elements similar to those found in the Gallican and Eastern Rites. The Gallican Rite itself, celebrated in modern-day France and Germany, with its dramatic and poetic character, as we saw in Chapter 1, demonstrated clear Eastern influence. There was also the Spanish Rite which has sometimes been called the Visigothic or Mozarabic Rite, exhibiting Gallican and Eastern influences once again. The British Isles knew what was called the Celtic Rite, but that came to be suppressed between the seventh and eleventh centuries due to Roman influence. Religious orders like the Dominicans and the Carmelites also had their own distinct rites. So the liturgical situation in the Christian West was anything but uniform prior to the Council of Trent.

Already in the third century, the *Apostolic Tradition* formerly attributed to Hippolytus of Rome offered general descriptions of liturgical rites with some texts,[1] and in the seventh century the *Ordines romani* introduced rubrics for papal Masses. The 1570 *Missale Romanum* of Pius V incorporated the rubrics from the 1501 *Ordo Missae* of the Papal Master of Ceremonies John Burckard of Strassburg, along with fifteenth-century material from papal liturgies. For example, at the request of Pope Innocent VIII (+1492), Agostino Patrizi Piccolomini and Burckard prepared a ceremonial which they presented to the Pope in 1488 and which was printed for the first time in 1516.[2] The Tridentine Mass was essentially the Medieval Rite with the elimination of medieval accretions, and the 1570 *Missal* was closely related to the *Missale Romanum* of 1474. However, unlike the 1570 *Missal*, the 1474 text contained few rubrics for the celebration of Mass. The first of the introductory sections in the *Missal* of Pius V was entitled 'General Rubrics of the Missal,' which included an overview of the Order of Mass as well as general norms about the ranks of feasts, choice of Mass texts, the time for celebrating Mass, the color of vestments, the preparation of the altar and other related topics. The second section was entitled 'The Rite to be Observed in the Celebration of Mass.' It gave detailed instructions for the priest and the server about how to celebrate Mass – instructions which found their origin in the *Ordines Romani*. The *Missal* itself differed little from the one used by Pope Innocent III between 1198 and 1216.[3]

At the turn of the sixteenth century, Burckard explained his rationale for including a full set of rubrics in his *Ordo Missae*:

> Engaged from my youth in the sacred ceremonies, when I saw that not a few priests in the celebration of Mass frequently imitated many abuses, and diverse rites and unsuitable gestures, I thought it unworthy that there is no definite norm transmitted to the priests by the holy Roman Church, Mother and teacher of all the churches, to be universally observed in the celebration of the Mass.[4]

Since Burckard's 1501 rubrics were intended for Mass with a congregation, they needed to be sufficiently re-worked for the 1570 *Missale* so that the basic texts described a 'private Mass' – normative within the Tridentine Rite. Thus, even when there was a congregation present, the rubrics for the Tridentine Mass were those of a Mass without a congregation, with all references to participation by the assembly eliminated. In the practical order, this meant that the presiding priest had to recite the *Introit* even when the choir sang it, and had to recite the scriptural texts under his breath even while they were being proclaimed by the subdeacon and the deacon. The Tridentine *Pontifical* forbade the distribution of Holy Communion to the faithful during the Chrism Mass. In fact, Communion by the faithful was more the exception than the norm in this period and when there was Communion, it was normally distributed before Mass or after but almost never during. This is clearly demonstrated in 'The Rite to be Observed in the Celebration of Mass,' which indicates that the Communion of the people during Mass was apparently an afterthought with the reference: 'If anyone is to receive Communion during Mass;'[5] or 'If Communion occurs at a solemn Mass.'[6] Not surprisingly then, one of the bishops at the Council of Trent actually argued that it would be better not to have the faithful there at all since it was difficult to concentrate on offering the sacrifice when people came in late or were coughing and sneezing behind their backs!

Following the second section on 'The Rite to be Observed ...' there was a third section: 'Concerning Defects Occurring in the

Celebration of Masses.' This section listed the various types of problems that could occur during Mass and what the priest should do if they actually did occur. For example, it included instructions on what a priest should do if he discovered that water rather than wine had been poured into the chalice, but also defects regarding the disposition of the celebrant's soul and body as well as his intention in celebrating. Even in the 1962 edition of the Tridentine Missal there was a prayer to be said as part of the Thanksgiving after Mass, *Obsecro te, dulcissime Domine Iesu Christe*, 'I beseech you, most sweet Lord Jesus Christ,' in addition to the Prayers to the Blessed Virgin Mary and St. Joseph, St. Thomas Aquinas, and the saint whose memorial of feast had just been commemorated. That prayer included an introductory note: 'To the one who recites the following prayer on bended knees (unless impeded) there is conceded the remission of defects and faults committed through human frailty in the celebration of Mass.'[7]

It is extraordinary that the text of these introductory rubrical sections did not change substantially in the almost four hundred years between 1570 and the 1950s when the rites of Holy Week were reformed by Pius XII. Indeed, the above-mentioned text cites Pope Pius X as having provided the Introductory note on 29 August 1912, which refers to the indulgence granted by Pope Pius IX in 1846 for those priests who worthily prayed that prayer. A major revision of the first rubrical section did not occur until 1960 while the second section on 'The Rite to be Observed' was not reformed until 1965. These three initial sections delineated the rules and actions of the clergy and other ministers and were to be followed with precision.[8]

The Liturgical Reforms of the Second Vatican Council

That historical background is important as we attempt to under-stand the *General Instruction of the Roman Missal* after Vatican II, which sought rather to assist in fostering a proper choreog-raphy for worship. Nonetheless, both the Council of Trent and

Vatican II employed a common mode of reform, desiring to return to the ancient Patristic tradition and to the 'pure and classical Roman Rite.' The Second Vatican Council was clear to make the case that it was in continuity with the Council of Trent and this is well exhibited in Number 15 of the 2002 *Instruction*:

> the liturgical norms of the Council of Trent have certainly been complemented and perfected in many respects by those of the Second Vatican Council, which has brought to realization the efforts of the last four hundred years to bring the faithful closer to the Sacred Liturgy especially in recent times, and above all for zeal for the Liturgy promoted by Saint Pius X and his successors.

In fact, the current *General Instruction* notes that the *Roman Missal* of Paul VI brings to completion the Tridentine norms that were never properly implemented.[9]

At the same time, the Council's call to renewal and participation also offered a radical step forward from what had preceded it. We read in Number 50 of *Sacrosanctum concilium*: 'The rite of the Mass is to be revised in such a way that the intrinsic nature and purpose of its several parts, as also the connection between them, can be more clearly manifested, and that the devout and active participation by the faithful can more easily be accomplished.' Number 11 is even more direct: 'Something more is required than the laws governing valid and lawful celebration ... the faithful [should] take part fully aware ... actively engaged in the rite and enriched by it.' And finally, Number 14: 'Mother Church earnestly desires that all the faithful should be led to that full, conscious, and active participation ... which is demanded by the very nature of the liturgy.'

The 1969 Order of Mass included changes in the attitude of the assembly – presupposing participation; in the structures; and in the liturgical *locus*. The Opening Rites carried out at the presidential chair or bishop's *cathedra* include a public act of penitence or *Asperges*, and conclude with the Collect Prayer. The mere mention of a presidential chair is itself a novelty since there was none in the Tridentine liturgy.[10] The *locus* for the

Liturgy of the Word moves between chair and ambo: three readings on Sundays and feasts at the ambo; the Homily, Creed, and General Intercessions at the chair and ambo. The Liturgy of the Eucharist moves between the altar and chair while the Concluding Rites take place at the chair or the altar.[11]

There were some in the Roman Curia, particularly Cardinal Alfredo Ottaviani and Cardinal Antonio Bacci, who complained that the 1969 *GIRM* was a break in tradition. In response to the introduction of the New Order of Mass on 3 April 1969, the two cardinals joined by a small group of Roman consultors wrote a short critical study of the *novus ordo* which they submitted to Pope Paul VI several months later, on 25 September. In their covering letter, the cardinals wrote: 'the new order of Mass represents, both as a whole and in its details, a significant departure from the Catholic theology of the Mass formulated at the twenty-second session of the Council of Trent.'[12] This resulted in the addition of a *Preamble* in the 1970 General Instruction which spoke of the new text as: A Witness to Unchanged Faith (nos. 2–5); A Witness to Unbroken Tradition (nos. 6–9); and Accomodation to New Conditions (nos. 10–15).

The 1970 Instruction also revised some texts from the 1969 edition. For example, Number 55d of the 1969 text made no mention of the consecration and sacrifice but referred only to 'The Institution Narrative.' The 1970 edition read: 'The Institution narrative *and consecration*: by means of words and actions of Christ, *the Sacrifice* is carried out ...' The 1973 General Instruction omitted certain numbers from the 1970 Instruction (nos. 142–150) – for example, references to the subdiaconate since this had been suppressed by Paul VI in *Ministeria quaedam,* but adding references to the acolyte helping with Holy Communion.[13]

In the second edition of the *Roman Missal* and the 1975 *General Instruction*, sections referring to the ministry of readers and acolytes were added to take the place of the omitted 'subdeacon' paragraphs. There was a change in wording describing the gesture after the consecration from *elevatio* to *ostensio*, i.e. from elevating the paten and then the chalice to 'showing them to the people,' reserving the elevation for the

Doxology at the end of the Eucharistic Prayer: 'Through Him, With Him, and in Him …'.[14] Some rubrics were also clarified, for example naming the bishop in Number 109. New Masses and titles for Prefaces were also added. The promulgation of the 1983 *Code of Canon Law* prompted further emendations in the *General Instruction*, changing the text when it referred to the homily, concelebration, the altar, the tabernacle, the bread for Mass, and Masses without a Congregation, so that the *General Instruction* would more closely correspond to the text of the revised Code.

The 2002 *General Instruction of the Roman Missal*

A revised edition of the *General Instruction* was made public at the end of July 2000 – a preliminary version of what appears in the 2002 Latin typical edition of the *Roman Missal*. Interestingly, over 210 paragraphs out of 399 were changed between 2000 and 2002: some major, such as rewriting the beginning of a private Mass; some minor, such as capitalization, spelling, corrections, and other stylistic changes. Major changes were to apply both to the 2000 and 2002 texts.[15] The Congregation for Divine Worship and the Discipline of the Sacraments were quick to note that the new *Missal* and *General Instruction* is an evolution, not a shift.

Like the 1969 *General Instruction*, the 2002 text contained the same order of chapters and headings. Chapter 1 deals with 'The Importance and Dignity of the Eucharistic Celebration' (nos. 16–26); Chapter 2 with 'The Structure of the Mass, Its Elements and Its Parts' (nos. 27–90); Chapter 3 is entitled 'The Duties and Ministries in the Mass' (nos. 91–111); Chapter 4: 'The Different Forms of Celebrating Mass' (nos. 112–287); Chapter 5: 'The Arrangement and Furnishing of Churches for the Celebration of the Eucharist' (nos. 288–318); Chapter 6: 'The Requisites for the Celebration of Mass' (nos. 319–351); Chapter 7: 'The Choice of the Mass and Its Parts' (nos. 352–367); and Chapter 8: 'Masses and Prayers for Various Circumstances and

Masses for the Dead' (nos. 368–385). To these original eight chapters, the 2002 edition of the *General Instruction* adds a ninth chapter: 'Adaptations within the Competence of the Bishops and the Conferences of Bishops' (nos. 386–399).[16]

Chapters 1 and 2 offer the framework and context for subsequent chapters and, in particular, provide important background on the various elements of the liturgy. For example, we are reminded that 'When the Sacred Scriptures are read in Church, God himself is speaking to his people (no. 29); or that 'great importance should be attached to the use of singing in the celebration of Mass (no. 40). Moreover, Chapter 2 also provides an overview of the Mass, leaving the more specifically rubrical details to Chapter 4. Chapter 3 addresses the duties of the liturgical participants, giving special attention to the 'people of God' – the dominant ecclesiology operative within the Conciliar documents. This, once again, is a radical departure from what is found in the introductory sections of the 1570 *Roman Missal*, where participation by the liturgical assembly was not a consideration.

Chapter 4 presents the details about various forms of celebration: Mass with and without a congregation; Mass with and without a deacon; and information about Communion under both kinds. Chapter 5 deals with issues of liturgical design and the arrangement of furnishings. For example, 'the altar should be built free-standing to allow the ministers to walk around it easily and Mass is to be celebrated facing the people' (no. 299). The location of the tabernacle is also dealt with in this section.

Chapter 6 offers the specifics on the items needed for the Eucharist. Significantly, the text notes that even though the bread is unleavened, the 'meaning of the sign demands that the material for the Eucharistic celebration truly have the appearance of food' (no. 321). In this section which also treats the color of vestments and liturgical vessels, some material from the rubrical introduction to the 1570 *Missal* was retained. Chapters 7 and 8 deal with the particular Mass texts that are used and how best to choose when there are several options. Noteworthy is the admonition that 'in planning the celebration of Mass, then, the priest should pay attention to the common spiritual good of the people of God, rather than his own inclinations,' and that 'choices are to be made in consultation with those who perform some part of the celebration, including the faithful (no. 352). In other words, the Mass does not belong to the priest but to the people of God, and consequently there is a value to joint planning and preparation, including, I would add, in the homily preparation itself.

Chapter 9 offers a final section which treats local adaptations approved by episcopal conferences consistently with what is stated in the *Sacrosanctum concilium* 37–40 on cultural adaptation – what will later be called 'liturgical inculturation.' This final chapter is new – an addition to previous Instructions – and in many respects represents the fruit of the post-Conciliar liturgical renewal. We read at Number 390 that it is the competence of episcopal conferences to determine

> the gestures and posture of the faithful; the gestures of veneration toward the altar and the *Book of the Gospels*; the texts of the chants at the entrance; at the preparation of the gifts, and at Communion; the readings from Sacred Scripture to be used in special circumstances; the form of the gesture of peace; the manner of receiving Holy Communion; the materials for the altar and sacred furnishings, especially the sacred vessels, and also the materials, form, and color of the liturgical vestments.

Number 394 states that each diocese should have its own liturgical calendar and Proper of Masses, and bishops' conferences should establish a calendar either for the country or a geographical region of several countries, as is the case of the Episcopal Conference of Southern Africa which comprises an area larger than South Africa itself. Number 397 states that 'the Roman Rite has acquired a certain supraregional character;' thus, the *Roman Missal* 'must be preserved in the future as an instrument and an outstanding sign of the integrity and unity of the Roman Rite.'[17]

There were various categories of change introduced into the 2002 text and there were some significant editorial changes as well. For example, the priest no longer 'goes up' to the altar but rather approaches it. The readings are now proclaimed 'from' the ambo rather than 'at' the ambo. There were also various attempts to clarify language, for example regarding 'reverence' made toward the altar. Those references are now more explicit by substituting or including a 'profound bow' rather than a 'proper reverence' as stated in the older text. Liturgical ministries are now distinguished between 'sacred,' when referring to ordained ministers, and 'duly instituted,' when referring to the laity. Moreover, in several places the text now reads that the presider 'says or sings' where the earlier *Instruction* read 'he says.'[18]

The new *General Instruction* also attempted to correct inconsistencies found in earlier texts. For example, Chapter 2 in the previous edition failed to take into account the presence of the deacon in its description of parts of the Mass. That is corrected in the 2002 text, mentioning the deacon when appropriate and his function in relation to the other liturgical ministers and the Mass itself. Another omission in the 1975 *Instruction* was the lack of any reference to the blessing and sprinkling of the holy water in place of the act of penitence; that too is corrected in the 2002 text. The revised text now also makes reference to the Holy Spirit where the Father and Son are mentioned (nos. 16, 78, 79d) for greater consistency and heightening the Trinitarian dimension of the text and, indeed, of the liturgy itself. The 1975 *GIRM* was also inconsistent about mentioning the people's responses – a problem now corrected in the 2002 Instruction.[19]

The revised 1983 *Code of Canon Law* addressed various liturgical topics such as the bread and wine used for Mass; concelebration; the role of the homily; church architecture; and Eucharistic reservation. Those changes needed to be carefully considered in preparing the 2000 and then the 2002 *Instruction*.[20] There was also a new Rite of Dedication of a Church and Altar (1977); a new edition of the Lectionary (1981); a new Ceremonial of Bishops (1984); and other liturgical documents, which needed to be referenced in the New *Instruction*. Some significant changes came as a result: The altar is now affirmed as a symbol of Christ (no. 298) –

something to which I refer frequently in Rome when my students seem to think that the tabernacle is the only or most important object during the celebration of Mass. Silence during the Liturgy of the Word is now mentioned and, indeed, encouraged (no. 56). Details on incensing are included (no. 277). There is to be no tabernacle on the altar where Mass is celebrated (no. 315); and rules are now clearly established for flowers during Advent and Lent (no. 305).[21]

Equally interesting is the list of 'Omissions and Changes from Experience. For example, comments in the 1975 General Instruction about permitting women to proclaim the scripture readings have been dropped since their regular service as lectors is no longer considered an exception (no. 107); there was an enumeration of cases for Communion under both kinds (no. 242); the chalice veil, while called 'laudable' in the 2002 Instruction, is no longer required (no. 118); the 2002 GIRM now permits the homily to be given either at the chair or the ambo 'or another suitable place' (no. 136). At the invitation to Communion, the presider may, as an alternative to holding a piece of the host over the paten, hold it over the chalice (nos. 84, 157, 243, 268).

The 2002 General Instruction acknowledges that tabernacles are often found on old altars in sanctuaries (no. 315), sometimes centered behind the altar used for Mass (no. 310). Thus, it states that as an alternative to a separate Eucharistic chapel, the Eucharist may be reserved in the sanctuary, but it explicitly leaves the ultimate decision on Eucharist reservation to the diocesan bishop. The location of the tabernacle has certainly been one of the most hotly debated topics in the past twenty or thirty years. Prior to the 2002 Instruction, conservative lobbyists held out great hope that the new GIRM would set the record straight once and for all, and insist that every church place the tabernacle in the center of the apse. It did not. But when the tabernacle is placed directly behind the altar of celebration, the ministers are to genuflect toward it in the opening and closing processions. Otherwise during the rest of Mass they are to bow to the altar as a symbol of Christ. Tabernacles were initially kept in sacristies in the early Medieval period, then in the wall of sanctuaries and suspended above the altar in the form of a dove. The sacrament was then gradually reserved in lateral chapels apart from the space for Eucharistic celebration until the advent of Baroque architecture and Charles Borromeo's 1577 decree for the Church in Milan which insisted that the tabernacle was to be placed on the altar of sacrifice.[22] Newly constructed churches after Vatican II tended to build Sacrament chapels for private prayer and also to distinguish the tabernacle from the liturgical space, while older churches whether renovated or not often moved the Sacrament once again to a lateral chapel.[23]

Some discreet changes in the rules for Communion under both kinds can also be found in the new text, suggesting that the practice of offering the chalice to the lay faithful is a more widespread practice than was the case in earlier editions of the *Instruction*. In his commentary on the 2002 Instruction, Dennis Smolarski, S.J. notes that the 1975 *GIRM* (no. 242) listed fourteen cases when the chalice might be offered to the lay faithful at Mass, of course always with proper catechesis and the permission of the diocesan bishop. The 2002 *General Instruction* (no. 283) reduces that list to three, but the categories of those individuals who may drink from the chalice has increased despite the shorter list.[24] That said, however, there remains a huge divide between universal norms and local practice, and the tradition of offering the chalice to all members of the liturgical assembly is hardly universally established. While it is an increasingly common practice in much of North America and Oceania as well as in the United Kingdom, it is virtually unheard of in Italy, Portugal, and Spain, not to mention Asia, Africa, and South America. And on those rare occasions when Communion is distributed under both forms in those parts of the world, it is usually given by intinction – the minister dipping the host into the chalice, then placing the host on the tongue of the communicant.

There are also additions that do not change existing practice but explicitly note what should be done: for example, that the priest must receive Communion from what he has consecrated at that Mass (no. 83, cf. also 243). It is important to note, however, that this directive is put in the context of the faithful also receiving Communion from what has been consecrated at that same Mass, emphasizing even more strongly that one should not use the tabernacle as a Sacramental dispensary during liturgical celebrations unless absolutely necessary. As far back as 1742, Pope Benedict XIV (+1758) insisted that the Church stop using the tabernacle as a dispensary for Holy Communion during Mass. Rather, the faithful should communicate together with the priest from the same altar and the same sacrifice. That desire is keenly expressed in the new *General Instruction* although it continues to be the ignored in many parts of the world.

The 2002 *Instruction* states that it is desirable to celebrate Mass facing the people whenever possible (no. 299). Explicit mention is made of other priests, deacons, or extraordinary ministers who may assist the presider in distributing Communion (nos. 162, 182). There is also mention of what to do with the remaining Eucharistic elements: they may either be consumed or placed in the tabernacle (no. 163). A directive is given regarding who requests a blessing before proclaiming the Gospel: when there is no deacon at a concelebration at which a bishop is the principal celebrant, a priest who proclaims the gospel should ask a blessing of the bishop (no. 212). If, however, the principal celebrant is another priest, then the concelebrating priest proclaiming the gospel should not ask for a blessing. Then there are other additions that may change existing practice because of a broad interpretation of the earlier versions of the General Instruction. For example, the Lectionary should never be carried in procession (no. 120d), only the Book of the Gospels.

While the 1975 *Instruction* noted that the priest could extend the sign of peace to the ministers near him (no. 112), it became customary in many places for the priest to leave the sanctuary and greet some of the assembly. Indeed, in some places where I have worshiped, the presider has greeted *all* of the assembly! Be that as it may, the 2002 *GIRM* now states that the presider should not extend the sign of peace to those outside the sanctuary 'so that the celebration not be disturbed' (no. 154).[25] The history of the greeting of peace is quite interesting, and was often exchanged hierarchically from the altar especially in monasteries, with the main celebrant passing the peace to those immediately on his left and right.[26] They, in turn, passed the peace by order of rank to their neighbors. Even today in certain oriental rites the peace is only exchanged among the concelebrating clergy.

The current placement of the sign of peace was a significant point of discussion during the 2005 Synod on the Eucharist. A number of bishops and cardinals lamented the fact that the *Fractio Panis* is gradually assuming an inferior role to the peace since the greeting often continues throughout the *Agnus Dei* even after the priest has broken the host. This was reflected in the 'Final Propositions' which the Synodal bishops offered to Pope Benedict. The Holy Father took this recommendation into account in his post-synodal exhortation *Sacramentum Caritatis* (no. 49). He then suggests in the document that 'competent curial offices' study the possibility of moving the sign of peace. Last year that study was completed by the Congregation for Divine Worship and the Discipline of the Sacraments, and the proposal to shift the sign of peace to the end of the Liturgy of the Word as a bridge to the Liturgy of the Eucharist was considered by episcopal conferences around the world. The rationale for that placement cites the Matthean injunction: 'Before bringing your gift to the altar, go and make peace with your brother or sister.' In returning the sign of peace to that ancient position, the Roman Rite would join the Ambrosian Rite and various Eastern rites which place it there. Moreover, in the realm of ecumenical liturgical cooperation and in light of the loss of common texts with our new translations as we saw in the last chapter, it would offer an ecumenical bridge since Anglican and Lutheran Rites along with other churches, traditionally place the sign of peace at the conclusion of the Liturgy of the Word.

There are, of course, good theological and pastoral reasons for leaving the sign of peace where it is currently found in the Roman Rite – just before the *Agnus Dei* is chanted. But it also must be stated that situations where the greeting of peace has upstaged the *fractio panis* are not uncommon. I witnessed this last year in Kenya at a large parish in Nairobi, where a lengthy and rousing song at the sign of peace with the assembly clapping and swaying to the beat was followed by a rather uneventful

'Lamb of God,' recited and introduced by the presider. The *Instruction* also states that since the breaking of the bread reflects one of the key verbs used in the New Testament to describe the actions by Jesus at the Last Supper, the rite is now explicitly reserved for the priest and the deacon (no. 83).

Further additions reinforce the importance of proper liturgical style and practice. For example, the 2002 *General Instruction* includes new paragraphs that emphasize respect due to the altar as symbol of Christ, explicitly noting there should be no flowers on top of the altar (nos. 305–306) – a message that has not yet reached Italy or Spain! And the readings should be proclaimed from the ambo even during private Masses (no 260). The practice of the assembly joining the priest in praying the doxology at the end of the Eucharistic Prayer is not to be permitted. This was a mistaken practice that grew in the years after the Council by well-intentioned priests who, failing to understand what was meant by 'full, active, and conscious participation,' invited their assemblies to join in praying the doxology. Indeed, in the years immediately after Vatican II, there were some churches in the Netherlands and elsewhere where the assembly was invited to pray the entire Eucharistic Prayer aloud with the priest. The 2002 *Instruction* now states at no. 147: that 'The Eucharistic Prayer demands, by its very nature, that the priest alone speak it' (no. 147), and that 'The concluding doxology of the Eucharistic Prayer is spoken solely by the principal priest celebrant and, if desirable, together with the other concelebrants, but not by the faithful' (no. 236). This is not an attempt at clericalism or to deny the lay faithful their right to participate, but rather a matter of good liturgical sense. Already in the year 150 CE, Justin Martyr in his First Apology affirmed the importance of the people's great 'Amen' as a grand assent to all that the president had proclaimed in the Eucharistic Prayer. Obviously, the 'Amen' loses its vigor if there is no one to proclaim it.

We also find some new practices included in the 2002 *GIRM*, such as the Bishop's blessing the people with the Gospel Book (no. 175) – a practice first introduced in the Roman Rite by Pope John Paul II during papal liturgies both in Rome and abroad, and also found in some usages of the Byzantine Rite. Moreover, as an alternative to the triple swinging of the censer, the priest is permitted to incense the bread and wine at the Preparation of the Gifts by making a single sign of the cross over the gifts with the censer (no. 277). The new *Instruction* also contains alterations of the current law. For example, the Psalm after the First Reading must not be substituted; the presider may sing all of the Eucharistic Prayer and not only the words of institution; the beginning of the private Mass now follows the rubrics of Mass with a congregation, including going to the chair and using an ambo or lectern.[27]

Future Considerations: Opportunities for Catechesis

From the outset, it should be stated that the 2002 *General Instruction* does not contain many changes. In other words, this text is a refinement of earlier editions of the *Instruction* and not a radical shift as happened in 1970. But it does provide a needed opportunity – an invitation – to look at how the Eucharist and other sacraments are celebrated in our parishes and dioceses. As the universal Church prepares to receive and implement the new liturgical translations in the coming years, reflection upon the new *General Instruction* might help to offer a context for looking at the bigger picture – a prayerful and thoughtful consideration of our liturgical practice within our respective dioceses and regions. Such reflection, I believe, could assist local churches in promoting a solid catechesis on the new liturgical texts which finds a firm foundation within the 2002 *General Instruction*.

As I have stated already, liturgy and ecclesiology are intimately linked and this is especially evident within the liturgical celebration itself. The ways in which the assembly moves together as one body communicates something quite powerful about the unity within Christ's Church. If we take the ancient liturgical principle of *lex orandi, lex credendi* to heart – that the liturgy proclaims all that the Church believes and teaches – then unity within the liturgical celebration symbolizes and articulates that unity inherent within the Mystical Body of Christ. At the same time, it offers a foretaste of the fullness of that communion we shall experience at the eternal banquet. This is obviously a foundational notion that undergirds the need for a *General Instruction* in the first place – the need for a liturgical choreography as I mentioned earlier so that the liturgical assembly is capable of moving together as one body. John Burckard recognized that need back in 1501; five hundred years later, that need is greater than ever. There are two intertwined sub-themes at play here. First, that the assembly is more than individuals in the same place at the same time; and second, that corporate worship is not simply another form of private prayer carried out in common.

Our liturgical assemblies run the risk of falling into the same trap as their non-religious cultural counterparts in settling for the sort of rampant individualism and competition so typical of contemporary culture. Forty-five years on, it remains very difficult to convince people that worship in the liturgical assembly is about the bigger picture – God's mission within the world and our role within it – something much larger and richer than one's personal piety or salvation. This problem is not limited to the laity, but can be just as present when clergy view the Mass as their own personal devotion. Of course, personal piety is to be respected, but we need to remain vigilant that such piety not overshadow corporate liturgical prayer as Christ's mystical body sent forth on mission. This includes common postures during the liturgy – all kneeling or standing or sitting at the same moment. It also includes entrance, offertory, and communion processions when members of the assembly walk together so as to demonstrate their unity within Christ's body. The recently introduced practice at papal Masses in which a select group of about thirty people are made to kneel when receiving Communion from the Holy Father – and to receive on the tongue – while the other 5,000 participants may receive standing and in the hand should they so choose, has raised concerns among some bishops and liturgical scholars about just what sort of message is being communicated here – especially given the already massive challenges in fostering liturgical unity.[28] The *General Instruction* states at Number 42: 'The uniformity in posture to be observed by all participants is a sign of the unity of its members of the Christian community gathered for the Sacred Liturgy.' And again at Number 96: 'This unity is beautifully apparent from the gestures and postures observed in common by all the faithful.'

Careful attention to what the *General Instruction* offers is a helpful corrective to the numerous forms of individualism that threaten the unity of the liturgical assembly, evidenced, for example, in those who see no need to remain until the end of the liturgy and leave after Communion; or those who feel no need to say the prayers or sing the hymns with the rest of the congregation. Any liturgical celebration must start with the coming together of Christians who desire to form a unified assembly of believers. This is the foundation on which the celebration builds – that the liturgical assembly gathered by Christ to worship God the Father, is the primary and foundational image of God's Church.

As I mentioned earlier, the 2002 *Instruction* also offers an important opportunity to redress the balance in our desire to recover a sense of mystery and the transcendent. Critics of the liturgical reform often note that the post-Conciliar has become too banal and wordy – often times more didactic catechesis than worship, with commentaries and explanations on the various parts of the Mass. As stated in the second chapter, we must honestly admit that such a critique is not without merit. As we have seen, the Roman Rite has existed for centuries and can function quite well on its own when we stay out of the way and let the Rite speak for itself. In other words, I remain a firm adherent to the principle 'less is more,' especially regarding our liturgical practice. This is in no way to deny the importance of liturgical inculturation and proper contextualizing of the Roman Rite as it is celebrated in unique and varied places and circumstances. But those of us who preside at the liturgy need to do so prayerfully, with transparency and a careful custody of words, so that the 'genius of the Roman Rite' of which Edmund Bishop spoke in 1899 might be appreciated yet again, even in our own day.

An example is in order. In one of the Jesuit communities where I lived, there was one priest who consistently began Mass: 'May the *special* grace of our Lord Jesus Christ … be with you.' And I wondered: 'Now, how is the *special* grace different from the "grace of our Lord Jesus Christ"?' Another presidential problem for some members of the clergy is that of giving several homilies during Mass beginning with the Introduction: 'Good Morning Everybody.' And after several minutes of Introduction, he then continues: 'So now, let us begin as we begin every day of our lives, In the Name of the Father …' But we actually began the Mass five minutes ago with 'Good Morning' – a secular greeting that pales in comparison to one of the Pauline greetings – and the people are exhausted before they have even reached the first reading! Similarly announcements such as 'Please stand; please be seated' can easily be communicated non-verbally with a simple gesture of the hand. Moreover, attention to silence and the non-verbal is not helped by those who read aloud the rubrics or directives: 'The First Reading, A Reading from the Book of the Prophet Isaiah;' or 'Responsorial Psalm: The Lord is my light and my salvation. Together: The Lord is my light …'

Another presidential problem is found among those who need to introduce the readings with commentaries – a sort of 'coming attractions,' implying that the liturgical assembly is incapable of understanding what the reader is proclaiming. Indeed, it is with good reason that the *General Instruction* does not call for such introductions before each reading. The purpose of the homily, of course, is to break open God's Word and unearth the kernel of wisdom emerging from the scriptural texts which the Church offers us for that day. If there is a problem in grasping the proclaimed Word, then it would be better to attend to careful training of the readers themselves and their own unique and privileged role in proclaiming that Word so that it is grasped and understood by the assembly.

The Mass is further encumbered with additional words when presiders recite aloud the apologetic prayers clearly meant to be prayed in silence since they refer to the devotion and piety of the particular priest or bishop presiding and not that of the whole community: 'Lord, wash away my iniquity, cleanse me of my sin' or the priest's prayer before communion. Some priests, in their desire to be inclusive, change the singular into the plural: 'May the body and blood of Christ bring *us all* to everlasting life.' In such cases, our attention to mystery and the transcendent is further compromised along with our liturgical symbols themselves, and in making our worship more loquacious it is further impoverished.

A helpful remedy, of course, is attending to silence where it is called for in the *General Instruction*. The Roman Rite actually offers a number of places throughout the Liturgy where silence is possible, indeed encouraged. While we have made progress in this regard since the Council – observing silence after the first reading and Psalm, after the Second Reading and after the Homily – I believe that we still have a long way to go. The *General Instruction* invites silence in the Penitential Rite, after the presider's introduction and before the common confession of sin. Or in the Collect Prayer, precisely to reinforce or enhance that call to unity within the liturgical assembly: 'Let us Pray,' then the rubric 'Pause for silent prayer' before continuing on to pray the Collect itself. Or in the case of the Gospel Acclamation where the rubrics state that if the Alleluia is not sung, it may be omitted. The recitation of 'Alleluia, Alleluia' before the Gospel, in my opinion, is one step away from attempting to recite 'Happy Birthday to you.' It is either sung, or an equivalent verbal greeting is offered!

The Liturgy of the Eucharist offers its own recommended moments of silence. We find one example in the Offertory Prayers at the Preparation of the Altar and Gifts. Of course, they are beautiful prayers – 'Blessed are you, Lord God of all Creation' – and I am not suggesting that they should never be used, but the *General Instruction* gives the option that these prayers may be prayed in silence. Indeed, there are times when this is a welcome gift, for example at an early morning weekday Mass. Moreover, the moment preceding the Prayer After Communion offers a final opportunity during Mass. In my parish experience, it is often the case that Communion Song may run longer than expected. Immediately upon its conclusion, the presider rises and says 'Let us pray,' rather than observing the rubric which calls for silent meditation before that post-Communion prayer or again, after the words 'Let us Pray.' Oftentimes, I suspect, the priest is concerned about not keeping people waiting any longer since they might well have returned to their places in the liturgical assembly some time ago. But forfeiting that moment of silent prayer becomes yet another missed opportunity to enter into the mystery of Christ and be united together in silence before we are dismissed. In this regard, I believe that we have much to learn from the monastic liturgy and its careful attention to liturgical silence from the moment one enters the sacristy to vest for the celebration.

Conclusion

As we have seen, far more than a set of rigid rubrical directives, the 2002 *General Instruction of the Roman Missal* contains a rich theology of worship whose heart is the paschal mystery of Christ, the chief liturgist. Indeed, the *Instruction* reminds us that the Eucharistic celebration is always the action of the risen Christ. The Church participates in that action as members of Christ's mystical body, but the Eucharist is first and foremost God's gift to the Church. Cardinal Godfried Danneels, Archbishop of Mechelen-Brussel, states it very well when he writes that the liturgy 'is first "God's work on us" before being our work on God.' The alternative, Danneels notes, 'would become nothing more than the community celebrating itself.'[29] The *General Instruction* reveals that vision of the People of God beautifully arrayed, each with his or her proper place with a role and function to be exercised, because each one shares in the priesthood of Jesus Christ through baptism. Under the leadership of the diocesan bishop whom the *Instruction* calls the 'moderator, promoter, and guardian' of the liturgical life within the local church (no. 22), that vision of the People of God hierarchically ordered in a diversity of liturgical ministries is brought to full stature.

Some episcopal conferences and diocesan offices of worship are using this moment in our history to do the liturgical catechesis that we did not have the leisure to do in the years immediately after the Second Vatican Council. In other words, they are taking the 2002 *General Instruction* and new liturgical texts which we will be discussing in the next chapter as a sort of *kairos* moment – a fresh opportunity for the Church to be renewed in its worship of the triune God. I believe that the Church is offering us an important invitation here honestly to evaluate our liturgical practice and to reflect on how we can better improve our worship, so that it more profoundly exhibits the ecclesiological, liturgical, and theological vision of the Second Vatican Council. We now turn to the final chapter in which we will consider the proposed liturgical changes in the forthcoming English translation of the third edition of the *Roman Missal*.

Notes

1   See Paul F. Bradshaw, Maxwell E. Johnson, and L. Edward Phillips, *The Apostolic Tradition* (Minneapolis: Fortress Press, 2002).

2   Éric Palazzo, *A History of Liturgical Books* (Collegeville: The Liturgical Press/Pueblo, 1998), 234.

3   John Harper, *The Forms and Orders of Western Liturgy from the Tenth to the Eighteenth Century* (Oxford: Clarendon Press, 1996), 156–165.

4   Quoted in Nathan D. Mitchell and John F. Baldovin, *Institutio Generalis Missalis Romani* and the Class of Documents to Which It Belongs,' in Edward Foley, Nathan D. Mitchell, and Joanne M. Pierce, eds., *A Commentary on the General Instruction of the Roman Missal* (Collegeville: The Liturgical Press/Pueblo, 2007), 20.

5   *Ritus Servandus in Celebratione Missae*, Pt. 10, no. 6, '*Si qui sunt communicandi in Missa, paulo antea ministrans campanulae signo eos moneat*,' *Missale Romanum Anno 1962 Promulgatum* (Roma: CLV, 1994), LXII.

6   *Ritus Servandus* no. 9, '*Si in Missa solemni fiat Communio, omnia serventur, ut supra, sed prius communicet diaconum et subdiaconum, deinde alios per ordinem*,' *Missale Romanum*, LXIII.

7   *Missale Romanum*, LXXVIII.

8   Dennis C. Smolarski, S.J., *The General Instruction of the Roman Missal, 1969–2002: A Commentary* (Collegeville: The Liturgical Press, 2003), 7–8.

9   Gerard Moore, *Understanding the General Instruction of the Roman Missal* (New York: Paulist Press, 2007), 26–27.

10 See the unpublished doctoral dissertation on this subject by Daniel McCarthy, O.S.B., 'The Chair for the Ministry-Gift of Presiding in the Assembly and Directing the Prayer: Four Models and a Single Vision,' defended at the Pontifical Liturgical Institute in June, 2008.

11 Smolarski, 10–11.

12 *Breve esame critico del 'Novus Ordo Missae'* quoted in Annibale Bugnini, *The Reform of the Liturgy 1948–1975* (Collegeville: The Liturgical Press, 1990), 284–285.

13 Smolarski, 21–22.

14 Paul Turner, *Let us Pray: A Guide to the Rubrics of Sunday Mass* (Collegeville: The Liturgical Press/Pueblo, 2002), 116, no. 571.

15 Smolarski, 27.

16 For a thoughtful analysis of the ecclesiological, pastoral, and theological implications found within the 2002 *GIRM*, see the commentary published by members of the Catholic Academy of Liturgy: *A Commentary on the General Instruction of the Roman Missal* (Collegeville: The Liturgical Press/Pueblo, 2007).

17 No. 399.

18 Smolarski, 28.

19 Smolarski, 29–30.

20 Smolarski, 23–24.

21 Smolarski, 30–31.

22 See Caroli Borromei, *Instructionum Fabricae et Supellectilis Ecclesiasticae* (Libri II), Città del Vaticano: Libreria Editrice Vaticana, 2000).

23 Smolarski, 31–32.

24 Smolarski, 32.

25 Turner, 164–165.

26 See Keith F. Pecklers, S.J., 'Pray for the Peace of Jerusalem: Liturgy and Peace in Context,' *East Asian Pastoral Review* 43/3 (2006), 224–235.

27 Smolarski, 34–35.

28 See Monsignor Kevin W. Irwin, 'Which Liturgy is the Church's Liturgy?' *Origins* 38/37 (February 26, 2009), 582.

29 Cardinal Godfried Danneels, 'Liturgy Forty Years After the Second Vatican Council: High Point or Recession,' in Keith F. Pecklers, S.J., ed., *Liturgy in a Postmodern World* (London: Continuum, 2003), 9.

On the Reception and Implementation of the Third Edition of the *Roman Missal*   5

Introduction

In this final chapter we shall consider the issue of reception and implementation of the new liturgical translations. As already mentioned, one of the problems with the current *Sacramentary* is that it was produced in only four years – a project done in haste, incapable of rendering proper translations of the Latin in proclamable English as a result. In the current process of translating the third edition of the *Missale Romanum,* the International Commission on English in the Liturgy (ICEL) has been very careful to work in a painstaking manner so that the same mistakes are not made again, especially since the Church in the English-speaking world will be using the new *Missal* for the foreseeable future.

As always, context is important as is the process in which these texts were reworked through consultation with ICEL-member episcopal conferences. From a brief history of the translation process since the publication of *Liturgiam authenticam,* we will explore the role played by the various episcopal conferences in the revision of earlier drafts and consider the new translations themselves. Third, we will examine some of the particular challenges faced by the ICEL translators in their desire to render faithful translations of the Latin original while at the same time produce proclamable texts in English. We will then consider the more significant changes in the forthcoming *Missal,* before concluding the chapter with some reflections on the tasks of catechesis and implementation of the new texts.

With the publication of *Liturgiam authenticam* in 2001, followed by third typical edition of the *Missale Romanum* in

2002, ICEL began work immediately on producing a base text of an English translation of the Latin *Missal* which the ICEL translation team could work with. Nine review teams then examined what had been produced, commenting both on how faithfully the Latin text had been rendered in the vernacular, and on the feasibility or functionality of the text within the context of liturgical prayer. From the work of the review teams and the comments received, the base text was revised and came to be called the 'Proposed Text.' ICEL then formed a Roman Missal Editorial Committee which worked with the Proposed Text, making stylistic changes, adjustments in syntax and vocabulary, as well as revisions to improve the texts' proclamability. The results of the Editorial Committee's work produced yet another version of the Proposed Text.

When the ICEL bishops finally met in plenary session, they had in their hands not only the Latin text, but also the original base text which had been produced along with the revised text and the Editorial Committee's text. The bishops examined each text according to the principles established in *Liturgiam authenticam* – looking for theological accuracy and faithfulness to the Latin original on the one hand, but also a pastoral functionality on the other, keeping in mind that the texts would need to function in diverse cultural contexts within the English-speaking world.[1]

The Role of Episcopal Conferences in Refining Earlier Drafts

Each of the eleven member conferences within ICEL has a bishop representative who serves on the International Commission. In addition to the Executive Secretary of ICEL who is not a bishop, along with ICEL staff members, they are assisted by the expertise of Latinists and other scholars who produce the actual translations. After various drafts and revisions, when ICEL has finally agreed on a text, it is sent as a 'Green Book' to the ICEL member episcopal conference. Each bishops' conference independently determines how widely it will consult on the text beyond the bishops themselves. Individual bishops are always free privately to consult their own advisors and diocesan liturgy directors to make better informed decisions and recommendations. Thus, there was a Green Book for the Order of Mass, another for the Proper of Seasons, and a third for Ritual Masses. The bishops of each conference then forwarded their results to their conference's liturgical office which collated the materials received and produced a summary for the bishops. Those results were then sent to ICEL, which returned to the drafting table, attempting to re-work their texts according to the comments and criticisms received by the bishops.

After those revisions, a final text is then produced, called the 'Grey Book,' which is sent out to the ICEL-member episcopal conference once again for study and consultation. The Grey Book is then voted on by each individual episcopal conference within ICEL. Once those bishops have reached consensus, each conference submits its text separately to the Congregation for Divine Worship and the Discipline of the Sacraments for the needed *recognitio* or approval. By October 2008, thirteen Grey Books had been prepared and sent to ICEL episcopal conferences, at various stages of approval. The bishops' conferences do not necessarily move in step when voting on and approving the proposed texts. In some cases, one conference may approve a particular Grey Book while another rejects it or requests particular revisions before the bishops can reach consensus. In other cases, one conference's speed in approving a Grey Book can be to the detriment of another. For example, the Australian Bishops' Conference had not yet approved the Grey Book on the Order of Mass when the United States Bishops' Conference had already sent their text to the Congregation for the *recognitio*. The Australian bishops, in fact, had intended to request certain changes in the text before they could accept it. But they soon learned that they too had received the same *recognitio* for the Order of Mass without having asked for it, based on what the United States bishops had submitted. Within the Congregation itself, before reaching consensus on granting the *recognitio*, it consults its advisory body *Vox Clara*, discussed in

Chapter 3, which includes bishops from eight English-speaking countries.

While ICEL regularly invites feedback from individual bishops within member conferences, those results can be somewhat uneven with a certain decrease in respondents moving from the Green Book to the final draft of the proposed texts found within the Grey Book. In the United States, for example, despite an episcopal conference which numbers more than three hundred, only eight bishops chose to respond and make recommendations on the proposed texts in one of the Grey Books. At least in the American case, it is difficult to assess the poor response to the request for feedback. A number of bishops spoke of fatigue in having been at this process for so many years – first regarding the English translation of the second typical edition of the *Roman Missal* which never saw the light of day, and now with the work on the third edition. Others expressed a certain frustration at the fact that the recommendations they had made on changes in the Green Book went unheeded. Be that as it may, some bishops did respond to the request for comment on the various editions of the Grey Book, and at least some changes were made according to their evaluation and criticisms. As we move toward the eventual publication and implementation of the new *Missal*, the translations are much improved as a result of the bishops' comments and criticisms.

In a letter to the Presidents of the various English-speaking episcopal conferences dated 28 June 2007, Bishop Arthur Roche, the ICEL Chairman, wrote specifically about the 2006 Draft English translation of the *Proprium de tempore* which then became the revised Grey Book. Bishop Roche noted that the majority of comments focused on vocabulary and syntax, and explained how the bishops' comments influenced subsequent revisions leading to the publication of the Grey Book. In that letter, Roche admitted that a number of bishops wrote that ICEL had 'too often used words that are unfamiliar to the majority of Catholics.' One month after Bishop Roche's letter, in July 2007, I was interviewed on the BBC together with Archbishop Dennis Hart of Melbourne, Australia, during the ICEL meeting in Northern Ireland. In that interview, I raised the example of the term 'the inviolate Virgin Mary,' asking how many Catholics would be able to grasp the meaning of 'inviolate.' The Archbishop responded that just that morning after much discussion, they had struck the word 'inviolate,' replacing it with 'ever virgin' – clearly a much more accessible term. In fact, Bishop Roche's letter affirms that the Commission sought to pursue a middle course, replacing uncommon words with common ones as the example just given. 'But this process can go too far,' he cautioned, 'with the result that a well-known word becomes over-used.'[2]

Second, Bishop Roche observed that 'commentators found some of the prayers too contorted in their syntax, and some too long.' So the Commission went back to the drafting table once again and attempted to solve that problem. They tried to do so by 'removing many parentheses and using word-order that is more natural in English,' following, once again, a middle course. I quote:

> If we were to adopt the most apparently natural word-order in every case, we would sometimes fail to reproduce the distinctive emphases of the original. Many Latin prayers place their climax in the final line: often we have followed this pattern, at the cost of a certain loss of colloquiality, to avoid a limp conclusion to the prayer in question.[3]

This same point was made by the Chair of the United States Bishops' Committee on Divine Worship, Bishop Arthur Serratelli of Paterson, New Jersey, in an address he gave in October 2008 to the Federation of Diocesan Liturgical Commissions in Milwaukee, Wisconsin. He noted that Latin orations, especially the Post-Communion prayer, tend to conclude with a strong teleological or eschatalogical point. Thus, ICEL translators have tried to be faithful to this principle. The Bishop used an example from Tuesday of the First Week of Lent:

> Grant us through these mysteries, Lord,
> that by tempering earthly desires
> we may learn to love the things of heaven.

Such use of inversion is characteristic of the *Roman Missal* in Latin. Serratelli noted that eighteen of the proposed Prayers after Communion or 14 percent use such inversions, and that the non-colloquial word order actually makes the assembly more attentive to the prayer.[4]

As Bishop Roche states above, one major criticism coming from not a few bishops throughout the English-speaking world was regarding the length of the prayers. In an article published in *America* Magazine, Bishop Donald Trautman of Erie, Pennsylvania, Former Chairman of the U.S. Bishops' Committee on Divine Worship, was explicit on this point:

> Will the assembly understand the fourth paragraph of the Blessing of Baptismal Water, which has 56 words (in 11 lines) in one sentence? In the preface of the Chrism Mass, one sentence runs for 10 lines. How pastoral are the new collects, when they all consist of a single sentence, containing a jumble of subordinate clauses and commas?[5]

Bishop Roche discussed the length of the prayers with the Congregation's Prefect, Cardinal Francis Arinze, who agreed that 'since the Commission's new texts have an overall respect for the distinctive form of the Latin oration, no harm would be done if some of the longest prayers were divided into two syntactic units.' Thus, the Commission revised texts accordingly as evidenced in the Collects for the Baptism of the Lord and the Evening Mass of the Lord's Supper.

Some Comments on the New Translations

It is interesting to note that five prayers in that Grey Book for the 'Proper of Seasons' have conclusions which do not match the Latin original. In the case of the Collect for Monday of the Third Week of Advent, for example, the English word order requires that the Son be named earlier in the prayer than in the Latin original, making 'Through our Lord ...' more appropriate.

The opposite is true in the Prayer Over the Offerings for the Morning Mass on 24 December. In this case the English word order requires that the Son be named later in the prayer than in the Latin original, thus making 'Who lives and reigns for ever and ever' a more fitting conclusion. The Prayer After Communion for the Solemnity of the Most Holy Trinity offers yet another example. Here, to accommodate a better English word order, the Trinity is named earlier in the translated prayer than in the original Latin. 'Through Christ our Lord' concludes the prayer, consequently, rather than 'Who lives and reigns for ever and ever.' The conclusions of several other prayers were also changed for reasons similar to those explained above.[6]

A second comment involves the recovery of biblical imagery within the prayer texts. Bishop Arthur Serratelli observed that the new texts have been re-worked in such a way that they strongly transmit the scriptural references that are inherent within the *Roman Missal*. He uses the example of the revised draft of the Collect for the First Sunday of Advent:

> Grant, we pray almighty God,
> that your faithful may resolve to run forth with
> righteous deeds,
> to meet your Christ who is coming,
> so that gathered at his right hand
> they may be worthy to possess the heavenly kingdom.[7]

The Latin text employs the word *occurrentes* – 'running to meet.' Yet the current text makes no mention of running:

> All-powerful God,
> increase our strength of will for doing good
> that Christ may find an eager
> welcome at his coming
> and call us to his side in the
> kingdom of heaven.

'Running the race,' of course, is a Pauline image.[8] That same prayer offers an example in which ICEL decided to retain the single sentence structure to the prayer. Clearly, that single sentence prayer is longer than we are accustomed to hearing in English. At the same time, however, it should be noted that it is the same length as the Opening Prayer currently in use in the French, Italian, and Spanish *Missals*.

The new translations also reflect a Patristic consciousness that is not always as consistently present in the current *Sacramentary*. The new translation of the Prayer after Communion on the Memorial of Saint Augustine, 28 August reads:

> May the partaking of the table of Christ
> sanctify us, we pray, O Lord,
> that, being made his members,
> we may be what we have received.

This rich image of becoming that which we have received is taken directly from Augustine's Sermon 227 on the Eucharist in which he links the Eucharistic assembly with the Eucharistic food placed upon the altar.[9]

Other texts have been revised with attention to cadence and rhythm. The Collect for the Third Sunday in Ordinary Time found in the current *Sacramentary* is one problematic text that needed reworking because of some rather problematic stresses: 'direct your love that is within us, that our efforts in the name of your son …'. Here *'that our "ef"'* is all stressed while *'forts in the name of your Son'* is all unstressed. Revised translations are trying to avoid such collocations, giving a more melodic flow to the English stresses. It could be argued that there are too many commas and capitalizations, but ICEL translators argue that it should be easier to read on the spot because of sense line and punctuation improvements.

The general structure of the Collects has also been the subject of much discussion and critique, and as a result, ICEL has made significant progress in rectifying the problem. For example, an early draft of the Collect for the Feast of the Visitation began:

> Almighty, everlasting God,
> who inspired the Virgin Mary to visit Elizabeth
> while bearing your Son in her womb …

They caught it. But

100

The problem was not that it was exactly clear whose womb was carrying the Son of God! The revised text now reads:

Almighty, everlasting God,
while the Blessed Virgin Mary
was carrying your Son in her womb,
you inspired her to visit Elizabeth ...

The proposed Collect for the Fourth Sunday of Advent offers a similarly complex structure, but already enjoys popularity as the concluding prayer of the Angelus:

Pour forth, we beseech you, O Lord,
your grace into our hearts,
that we to whom the incarnation of Christ your Son
was made known by the message of an Angel
may by his Passion and Cross
be brought to the glory of the resurrection.

If one looks carefully at the collection of proposed Collect prayers as a whole, a gradual improvement in the quality of the texts becomes evident, both in terms of their language as well as their proclamability. This, however, suggests that their overall quality still remains somewhat uneven despite the fact that some of the prayer texts are well crafted. Such unevenness within the body of Collect prayers reveals the fact that different translators were involved in the project, some of whom were more gifted or competent than their colleagues. Others, perhaps, felt more constrained by the need to translate literally from the Latin original, resulting in texts that flow less naturally in English.[10]

No doubt, the elevated style of these prayers will cause an adjustment in the way the presider speaks or chants them, and also in the way the assembly hears them. In fact, the prayers may well need to be proclaimed aloud beforehand and rehearsed by the presider, since they will not necessarily flow in a matter to which we are accustomed. Even where problems do remain, however, ICEL translators are optimistic that the length of the

Collects will be a non-issue once we begin using them. In other words, they believe that we shall become increasingly acquainted with such syntax and style as we grow comfortable with the texts.[11]

We can note some positive developments regarding the prefaces and Eucharistic Prayers. The prefaces will now conclude more strongly in a way that leads better into the Holy Holy. For example, 'forever singing to your glory' is one such conclusion. Another one is 'we sing the hymn of your praise and acclaim without end.' These phrases are deliberately signed to produce a good sound when sung. Most will agree that the new rendering in Eucharistic Prayer III 'from the rising of the Sun to its setting' as opposed to the current usage, 'from East to West,' is a major improvement. Like the earlier reference to the richer biblical imagery evident in the revised Collect for the First Sunday of Advent, this revision reflects the words found in the Book of Malachi 1:11: 'from the rising of the sun to its setting.' Moreover, the new text also adds clarity as to the meaning of the Latin original for those, like my Jesuit classmate at Berkeley, California, who were fond of improvising on the text: 'So that from east to west, from north to south …' as if the reference were about geography! While the problem of inclusive language does remain in Eucharistic Prayer IV, it needs to be said that a good deal of the exclusive language found in the current *Sacramentary* has been eliminated. '*Deus*' was rendered 'Father' in the *Sacramentary* because it was thought to add warmth to the prayers and especially to make it plain that the prayer was directed to the first person of the Trinity. While a more literal translation of the prayer may render the address of the Prayer to the Father less evident, it nonetheless will make the address to God more gender-inclusive.[12]

The Challenges for ICEL Translators

Without denying the frustration that has been registered with the proposed and already approved revised liturgical texts which we are considering in this chapter, the translators themselves have been in a certain bind: they are now obligated to translate according to the newly established principles laid out in *LA*. For example, *Liturgiam authenticam* implies that various attempts to replace 'man' in Eucharistic Prayer IV with the more inclusive 'we' or 'man and woman' is called an 'imprudent solution.' We read at Number 31:

> to be avoided is the systematic resort to imprudent solutions such as a mechanical substitution of words, the transition from the singular to the plural, the splitting of a unitary collective term into masculine and feminine parts, or the introduction of impersonal or abstract words, all of which may impede the communication of the true and integral sense of the word or an expression in the original text.

I quote this quite deliberately because it explains, at least to some degree, the rationale employed by the translators. They are well aware that a translation of Eucharistic Prayer IV produced in 2009 that continues to use what is now considered the exclusive term 'man' within common English usage means that the newly published text will be problematic or outdated even before the ink has dried! Sadly, I fear that this will place us in the situation in which we were before the textual revisions: either priests will avoid Eucharistic Prayer IV altogether because of the masculine references it contains, or they will begin altering the text *ad libitum* despite the fact that they are not permitted to do so. There is little that we can do about that now, however, and we must learn to live with the texts we have been given. It is not surprising that ICEL translators found work on Eucharistic Prayer IV to be one of the thorniest issues they had to deal with. In any event, the new translation of Eucharistic Prayer IV, which has now been approved, is certainly a marked improvement over earlier drafts of the text, despite the fact that usage of exclusive language remains. Of course, the text which the earlier ICEL had proposed for the translation of the second edition of the *Roman Missal* rendered a fine prayer, excising all exclusive masculine language. But it would never have never received the needed approbation by the Congregation for Divine Worship given the new regulations stipulated with *Liturgiam authenticam*.

So to do justice to ICEL and the work of its translators, they had little choice but to produce the final draft which we now have in our hands. Recently, the Congregation for Divine Worship informed ICEL that it does not want the word 'humankind' to appear in the *Missal*, presumably because it is considered to be a neologism. This is but one example of many where the Congregation has established the rules which ICEL must implement. On the local level there can be a tendency to put the blame on ICEL for the texts that have been produced, but, as I have tried to demonstrate here, the situation is far more complicated than what might appear at first blush.

Changes in the Third Edition of the *Roman Missal*

A word is in order of the changes that await us in this revised edition of the *Roman Missal*. There will be a change in the hand gesture for the blessing of such objects as ashes, candles, and water. The rubric will now read 'With hands extended.' Moreover, the Eucharistic Prayers for Reconciliation will now be able to be used with other penitential prefaces. Prior to the 2002 edition, it was not permitted to substitute the respective preface for Reconciliation I and II with another.

There will be a number of new feasts added in the new *Missal*, for example the Feast of the Most Holy Name of Jesus on 3 January (originally on 1 January); Divine Mercy on the Second Sunday of Easter; Our Lady of Fatima on 13 May; and the Most Holy Name of Mary on 12 September. There are also new saints on the universal calendar: for example, Rita of Cascia on 22 May; Apollinaris on 20 July; Teresa Benedicta of the Cross (Edith Stein) on 9 August; Padre Pio on 23 September; and Catherine of Alexandria on 25 November. There will also be local adaptations. For example, in the United States 22 January will be a Day of Penitence on the anniversary of Roe v. Wade and the legalization of abortion.

There will be a number of changes regarding solemnities and seasons, as well. For example, there will be Prayers over the People for each day of Lent as part of the Dismissal Rite. The Apostles' Creed which was normally used only in Masses with children is now encouraged for general usage especially during Lent and Easter, but it may be used on any Sunday or feast day through the year. Included will be a new Vigil Mass both for the Feasts of the Epiphany and the Ascension, just as there is for the Vigil of Pentecost. The washing of the priest's or bishop's hands will be included after the washing of the feet on Holy Thursday, and Eucharistic Prayer I – the Roman Canon – will be obligatory at that same Mass of the Lord's Supper. On Good Friday, the priest or bishop may remove his shoes for the veneration of the cross if he so chooses; the humeral veil will be required to be used at that same liturgy in bringing the Eucharist to the altar for the Communion Rite. At the Easter Vigil, the preparation of the paschal candle will no longer be optional and the chanting of 'Light of Christ' must now begin at the door of the church.

Moreover, the Ritual Masses will have new entrance antiphons; the scrutinies will be separated into three; there will be particular inserts for Eucharistic prayers; the Mass for the Sick will be used normatively when anointing takes place and two solemn blessings will be included. There are also several editorial changes involving Ritual Masses: *Viaticum* will now precede ordination; the institution of lectors and acolytes will be added along with the dedication of a church and altar. The Masses for Various Needs and Occasions will be re-arranged from four to three groups: church; public circumstances (combining civil and public needs); and various needs. And there will be new masses added. There will also be additional Votive Masses: Divine Mercy; Our Lord Jesus Christ, High and Eternal Priest; John the Baptist; and Peter and Paul.

Most notable and challenging will surely be some significant changes within the Order of Mass itself. In the Introductory Rites, the presider will use the more inclusive term 'communion of the Holy Spirit' rather than 'fellowship' in greeting the liturgical assembly to which all respond: 'And with your spirit.' While there have been a number of criticisms in dropping 'And also with you' in favor of 'And with your Spirit,' it should be noted that this has always been the case in most other language groups. One exception has been the Church in Brasil in which the people respond 'He is in our midst' to the presider's 'The Lord be with you.' However, the Brasilian translators are now under the same constraints as ICEL and other linguistic liturgical commissions to offer a more accurate translation of the Latin '*et cum spiritu tuo*.' When the *Confiteor* is used as the 'Penitential Act' as it will now be called, the people will confess that 'I have greatly sinned ... through my fault, through my fault, through my most grievous fault.' The Gloria has been translated differently as well, and the structure of the prayer will have changes from the current text.

The opening of the Niceno-Constantinopolitan Creed shifts from 'We believe' to 'I believe,' 'Of one being with the Father' has now been replaced by 'consubstantial with the Father.' This shift in terminology has been one of the most hotly debated subjects among the bishops of various conferences, expressing their deep pastoral concern about their people's ability to understand the significance of 'consubstantial.' Those bishops gathered at the Council of Nicaea in 325 C.E. wanted to affirm that Jesus was equal to the Father and of the same substance (*homoousion*). The Council of Constantinople affirmed the same truth in 381 C.E. and the term *homoousion* came to be rendered in Latin as *consubstantialem*. As 'consubstantial' is a more literal translation of the Latin, it was retained in the new translation despite pastoral questions to the contrary. Moreover, 'for us "men" and for our salvation' has been retained in the same Creed, contrary to the proposition that the word 'men' be omitted as has been done in the revised liturgical books of other churches. The phrase '... was born of the Virgin Mary' now reads 'Was incarnate of the Virgin Mary and became man' which matches more closely what has been prayed in the United Kingdom since the Council and is indeed the text used by Anglicans, Lutherans, and other Christians in their rendering of the same text.

The 'Prayer Over the Gifts' will now be called the 'Prayer Over the Offerings,' as a more faithful rendering of the term *'Super Oblata.'* The Preface Dialogue has been slightly altered, as well. The people's response to 'Let us give thanks to the Lord Our God' will now be 'It is right and just' – once again, as has been the case for years in the other major language groups: *'Cela est juste et bon'* in the French, etc. The *Sanctus* will now read 'Lord God of hosts' in lieu of 'power and might.' The Eucharistic Prayers will all be included: the two prayers for Reconciliation in the *Ordo missae* following Eucharistic Prayers I through IV; the Eucharistic Prayers for Various Needs and Occasions will be placed in one appendix and the Eucharistic Prayers for Masses with Children in a different appendix. There will be a number of new Prefaces, as well: one for martyrs; a new one for the Blessed Virgin Mary; one for ordinations and another for the dedication of church and altar.

A particularly delicate issue has involved the *pro multis* discussion – 'Shed for you and for many for the forgiveness of sins.' In July 2005, the Congregation for Divine Worship and the Discipline of the Sacraments in agreement with the Congregation for the Doctrine of the Faith wrote to the presidents of all episcopal conferences on the subject asking their opinion on how best to render the term in the vernacular languages: 'for the many' or 'for all' as has been the case since Vatican II. One year later, on 17 October 2006, the then Prefect of that Congregation, Cardinal Francis Arinze, wrote once again to the conference presidents and explained that after consultation, 'for the many' was considered a more faithful rendering of the Latin *pro multis* and bishops should begin preparing their dioceses catechetically for the eventual shift to the more ancient term that will appear in the new *Missal*.

Several reasons were given for a return to the older usage: the synoptic gospels make specific reference to the 'many' for whom Christ is offering the sacrifice; the Roman Rite in Latin has always said *'pro moltis'* and never *'pro omnibus'* in the words of institution regarding the chalice; the *anaphoras* of various Eastern rites (e.g., Greek, Syriac, Armenian, etc.) contain the equivalent of *'pro multis'* in their respective languages. Several other reasons were offered, including a closer adherence to the translation norms established by *Liturgiam authenticam*. As I work with the media I had a flurry of telephone calls and emails, and journalists immediately read intrigue into the shift: was this an attempt to undercut the teachings of the Second Vatican Council? Did the Pope wish to suggest that Christ did not shed his blood for all, but only for some? And what about ecumenical and interreligious repercussions from such a shift?' In conversations with Italian colleagues prior to Cardinal Arinze's definitive letter in October 2006, I was getting mixed reports: '*pro multis*' was in, '*pro multis*' was out. Some bishops and cardinals expressed their own concerns to the Holy Father about the potential fallout from such a shift – both within our own ranks but also how this would be perceived from the outside. But as the Cardinal noted in his letter, it has been instructive that many Eastern Rites have consistently employed '*pro multis*' in the words of institution found within their respective Eucharistic Prayers, along with those of Anglicans and Lutherans. The Memorial Acclamation 'Christ has Died, Christ is risen' has been replaced with 'We proclaim your death, O Lord, and profess your resurrection until you come again.' The second acclamation, 'Dying you destroyed our death,' has been eliminated while the third and fourth acclamations found within the current *Sacramentary* have been altered.

There will be only one possible invitation to the Lord's Prayer which reads: 'At the Savior's command and formed by divine teaching, we dare to say.' The Prayer itself remains unaltered as does the Concluding Acclamation, 'For the kingdom, the power, and the glory are yours' but the 'Deliver Us' prayer is re-translated.' The presider will now invite the assembly to Communion with the words taken from John's Gospel 'Behold the Lamb of God' rather than the more colloquial 'This is the Lamb of God.' It reads in full: 'Behold the Lamb of God, behold him who takes away the sins of the world. Blessed are those who are called to the supper of the Lamb.'

In addition to discussing re-positioning the greeting of peace to before the preparation of the gifts, bishops gathered at the 2005 Synod on the Eucharist discussed the possibility of including additional formulae of dismissal of the liturgical assembly that would better link to mission beyond the confines of the church building. That item found its way into the list of post-Synodal propositions. By way of response, the Holy Father agreed with that recommendation. In October 2008, Cardinal Francis Arinze reported that the pope had approved two additional formulae for the dismissal rite in addition to *Ite missa est*. The new phrases are 'Go and announce the Gospel of the Lord' or 'Go in peace, glorifying the Lord by your life.'

The Task of Liturgical Catechesis and Implementation

ICEL bishops and translators had originally projected a 2011 or 2012 release of the new *Missal*, given the complicated translation work, consultation and voting in various stages, and eventual *recognitio* granted by the Holy See. However, in December 2008, the Prefect of the Congregation for Divine Worship and the Discipline of the Sacraments, Cardinal Antonio Cañizares Llovera, issued a letter to the Episcopal Conferences of ICEL, expressing his desire that the process be expedited so that the English edition of the *Roman Missal* might be published by the end of 2010. This more immediate timeline now puts pressure on ICEL translators and bishops' conferences to meet the new deadline.

To further complicate matters, the Southern African Bishops' Conference mistakenly gave approval for the proposed texts to be used immediately in South Africa, Botswana, and Swaziland, creating no small confusion. The problem was not only that work on the *Roman Missal* has not yet been concluded and approved by the Holy See, but also that there was no proper catechesis done at the local level prior to introducing the new texts. As already mentioned in Chapter 2, most liturgical scholars today would agree that the fundamental problem with the implementation of the Vatican II liturgical reforms was the lack of proper catechesis to facilitate such implementation. In Southern Africa, when the new texts were introduced in late 2008, the result was predictably one of anger and confusion among the clergy and lay faithful alike.

The Congregation for Divine Worship and the Discipline of the Sacraments then asked the South African Bishops Conference to stop using the new texts until the entire process had been completed and the *Roman Missal* approved so that English-speaking churches throughout the world might proceed with the implementation together. Obviously, once such a door has already been opened, it becomes quite difficult to close it. Indeed, had the bishops suddenly halted use of the new texts having just introduced them, it would have probably caused even greater confusion and unrest, and further impeded the eventual implementation of the new *Missal*. So the Holy See conceded and allowed the new texts to continue being used, although the pastoral problems remain with clergy and parishioners not understanding the rationale for the new translations, thereby calling into question the Conciliar principle of 'reception'– how are the texts to be received by the people so that they are made their own. The situation in Southern Africa offers a valuable lesson to the rest of the English-speaking world, however, on the need for a very careful and well-prepared catechesis in several stages – a catechesis that has already begun in the United States and the United Kingdom with formational materials available on the websites of the respective bishops' conferences, along with simple answers to questions regarding the 'why' of new liturgical texts in the first place.

A important contribution to the ongoing task of catechesis and implementation of the new *Missal* is being made by the 'Leeds Group,' under the direction of the Bishop of Leeds, the Rt. Rev. Arthur Roche who also happens to serve as the Episcopal Chair of ICEL. The Leeds Group consists of a small number of international liturgical scholars and was founded by Roche in 2006. The scope of the project is to provide catechetical materials that can be used and adapted by each episcopal conference. The Leeds Group has met several times to develop the sequence of liturgical catechesis and to commission five foundational essays which will serve as a basis for the catechetical resource. In October 2007, the liturgy secretaries of the ICEL-member episcopal conferences met in Washington, D.C. to be informed as to the project's development and to strategize together about how the efforts of the Leeds Group might best be utilized in their respective episcopal conferences. In January 2009, the Leeds Group met in London, where it reviewed a proposal from the Australian educational resources supplier, *Fraynework,* on the eventual production of a DVD to further assist catechetical efforts on the implementation of the new *Missal. Fraynework*'s proposal was accepted and a DVD of ten to fifteen minutes will be produced to introduce the subject. A more detailed PowerPoint presentation will follow during which group facilitators may lead participants in a more detailed study of the area. Finally, those who wish to pursue further study would be offered the foundational essays in addition to further information on relevant links.

All of us – bishops, parish priests, directors of worship offices, liturgical scholars – will need carefully to consider the challenges we will face as we move toward implementation of the new *Missal* and the best strategies to be employed in the area of liturgical catechesis. This will be essential to reach the ultimate goal of proper reception of the new texts by the entire English-speaking Church. And as I have mentioned in talks I have been giving on the subject, it is not too early to begin giving serious thought to such catechesis and implementation. Indeed, it will be too late to wait until the new *Missal* in English is in our hands. It will also be important to allow sufficient time to adapt current musical settings of the parts of the Mass and create new ones. In fact, ICEL has already hosted two consultations on this subject: one in Washington and another in Chicago. Obviously, the Mass settings currently in use will need to be revised to conform to the new texts. Many of us take for granted the singing of popular Mass settings such as Marty Haugen's 'Mass of Creation' and Richard Proulx's 'Community Mass.' We know them from memory. But those settings along with many others will need to be revised and new settings composed. This will also require the publication of new hymnals and the revision of old ones. In general, parishes and dioceses will need carefully to consider the materials needed effectively to execute the implementation and the ways they will go about it, not to mention the finances of purchasing liturgical books, hymnals, and other worship aids.

The Catholic Academy of Liturgy in North America's recently published *Commentary on the General Instruction of the Roman Missal* will be another significant resource. While it is not addressed to parishioners as such, but rather to clergy and lay pastoral leaders, it is quite helpful in the preparation of such catechetical sessions in parishes or dioceses. It offers the text of the *General Instruction* in Latin and English along with a scholarly commentary on each number within the *Instruction*, replete with footnotes and bibliography, not unlike that produced by the Canon Law Society of America after the 1983 Code of Canon Law was promulgated. Moreover, the Catholic Academy of Liturgy has just embarked on a second Commentary which will treat the Order of Mass.

Aside from catechetical announcements in parish bulletins; pre-liturgical announcements or catecheses and even preaching on the new texts when appropriate within the homily itself, there will also be the need of evenings of liturgical formation on the parish and diocesan levels, where liturgical scholars might be invited to offer the necessary theological background and context for the new translations. In other words, our efforts at catechesis and implementation cannot be limited to communicating information or simply teaching and rehearsing the new texts with our parishioners. Rather, we will need to reach more deeply to the wellspring of our worship, offering a mystagogical approach in our liturgical formation that draws upon the rich theology found within *Sacrosanctum concilium*; the *General Instruction of the Roman Missal*; and indeed, the new liturgical texts themselves.

Put differently, at this moment in our history, in which the Church will soon offer us new texts with which to pray, we would do well to ask ourselves where we find hope as we move forward and how we can rediscover that deeper source that underlies true liturgical formation and catechesis. Forty-five years after the promulgation of *Sacrosanctum concilium* we are being invited to ask deeper questions far beyond the practicalities or the obligation of implementing a new *Missal* given to the

Church. The recently deceased Anglican liturgical scholar Thomas Talley once quipped that 'too many communities have already been brought to despair by the discovery that, having rearranged the furniture of the sanctuary and instituted an offertory procession, they still don't love one another.' As the 'true and indispensable source for the Christian life,' authentic liturgy and, indeed, authentic liturgical formation should lead to ongoing conversion and transformation both individually and corporately as the Body of Christ alive within God's world.

Conclusion

If we have learned anything from the last time we had to implement new liturgical texts back in the 1960s and 1970s, this process of reception and implementation will not occur overnight. Indeed, if we want the process to be effective and if we wish the texts to take hold, we will need to take time to ponder them, dwell with them, pray with them, and let the words of those texts wash over us. Language is a living entity. It continues to evolve and change, and ourselves with it. Cardinal John Henry Newman once wrote: 'To live is to change. And to be perfect is to have changed often.' The new *General Instruction* and the new liturgical texts themselves are important because they are yet another call to Christians – ordained and lay alike – to reflect on the Church as the 'sacrament of unity' (*GIRM* 93) by sharing in the reality that makes the Church through the sharing of the one bread and the one cup. The new *General Instruction* and the new liturgical texts invite us to reflect on our common prayer and on how well we react to the symbolic nature of the liturgy.

At the end of his address to the Federation of Diocesan Liturgical Commissions, Bishop Serratelli offered some honest words of wisdom as we move toward the eventual implementation and reception of the new liturgical texts: 'The new *Missal* will come as the result of years of growth and understanding. It will improve our liturgical prayer, but it will not be perfect.

Perfection will come when the Liturgy on earth gives way to that of Heaven where all the saints praise God with one voice.'[13] Of this we can be sure: this will not be the last *General Instruction* nor will these new translations be the final word on Catholic Worship in the English-speaking world. But they *are* the texts which the Church is offering us now in our own day, to enrich our prayer and the life of the Church. May we receive them in faith, so that our worship of God in spirit and in truth may send us forth to live as more effective instruments of God's saving mission within the world so desperately in need of it.

Notes

1   Bishop Arthur Serratelli, 'Address to the 2008 National Meeting of Diocesan Liturgical Commissions,' 13 October 2008, Milwaukee, Wisconsin, in 'Newsletter: United States Conference of Catholic Bishops Committee on Divine Worship' (October 2008), 37.
2   Unpublished letter of Bishop Arthur Roche to the Presidents of the English-Speaking Episcopal Conferences, 28 June 2007.
3   *Ibid.*
4   Serratelli, 38.
5   Donald W. Trautman, 'How Accessible Are the New Mass Translations?' *America* (21 May 2007), 10.
6   *Ibid.*
7   Serratelli, 38.
8   See 1 Corinthians 9:24–26; Galatians 2:2; 5:7; Romans 9:16.
9   Serratelli, 38.
10 Email of Paul Turner to the author, 3 July 2008.
11 Paul Turner, 'A New Roman Missal: What to Expect from a New Translation of Liturgical Texts,' *America* (26 May–2 June 2008), 14–16.
12 Email of Paul Turner to the author, 3 July 2008.
13 Serratelli, 39.

Conclusion:
The Future of Liturgy
is the Future of the Church

6

In December 2007 at Archbishop's House, Westminster, London, Archbishop Piero Marini launched his new book: *A Challenging Reform,* discussed in Chapter 3. In the course of his remarks, the Archbishop made a rather bold statement: 'The Future of Liturgy is the Future of the Church.' The following morning during a press conference around the book's publication, he expanded on what he meant by those words:

> Celebrating the liturgy is itself the primordial source of renewal in the Church. We learn the liturgy by celebrating it. The more we succeed at celebrating the liturgy, the more we'll live the Christian life fully and the more we'll succeed in transforming the Church ... The great ideals of the Church are in crisis today in part because there's a crisis in the liturgy. The great ideals of ecumenism, of internal reform of the Church, are all connected. The crisis of the liturgy places in crisis these other great values, because the Council wanted to confront these challenges of the mission of the Church, or reform, of dialogue with the world, by beginning with the liturgy. If the liturgy is the source and summit, then we foster in the liturgy the kind of life we need to meet these great goals. If these great movements of the Church are in difficulty today, we have to look to the difficulty in the liturgy.[1]

Archbishop Marini's words are timely as we consider the ongoing evolution of the Roman Rite in the twenty-first century and as the third edition of the *Roman Missal* will soon be implemented in English. We must be vigilant that our projected liturgical catechesis not lose the bigger picture – liturgy's intimate link to ecclesiology, for example. And as I mentioned in the final chapter, we must also be vigilant in assuring that our formation not be limited to practical instruction on using the new *Missal*, but rather is a mystagogical approach which invites deeper reflection on the role that the Roman Rite plays in the life and mission of the Church. If our Catholic tradition realized and celebrated in worship is to be credible, capable of reading the signs of the times, then we will need to be courageous in asking those difficult questions about where our worship is leading us and what it is demanding.

Such mystagogical catechesis reminds us that authentic liturgy is infinitely richer than our liturgical texts and how we translate them. Like the rest of Christian worship, the reformed Roman Rite is always intended to lead to mission. The goal, then, is that the language of the Eucharist become the language and pattern of our own lives as we participate in God's mission within human society.[2] As Pope Benedict XVI notes in *Deus Caritas Est,* love of God and love of neighbor constitute one inseparable reality. That truth is celebrated *par excellence* in the Eucharist. The question before us is how our liturgical catechesis on the new translations and our eventual implementation of the third edition of the *Roman Missal* will help us to do this. The recently canonized Jesuit saint from Chile, Alberto Hurtado, often spoke of the 'prolongation of the Mass in daily life' – similar to that which the late Jesuit theologian Karl Rahner referred to as the 'liturgy of the world', and his fellow Jesuit Teilhard de Chardin spoke of as 'The Mass on the World.' It is not a coincidence that the word 'Mass' comes from *missio*. But that *missio* cannot be limited to the sending forth at the end of the Eucharist. The Roman Rite articulates *missio* from start to finish because liturgy and mission are woven together intrinsically just as are love of God and love of neighbour. Put differently, how we understand worship will determine how we understand mission.

As we have seen in this book, the Roman Rite has been adapted and contextualized since its very inception. The future of the Roman Rite will be determined by its continued capacity to be inculturated and contextualized in very diverse circumstances and situations, in a way radically different from 1963 when *Sacrosanctum concilium* was promulgated. But such contextualization in no way suggests that worship be self-referential. If our liturgical participation is only about us in this particular time and place, forgetting the rest of God's world especially where it is most in need, then the community will be celebrating nothing more than itself – a sort of 'liturgical isolationism.' On the other hand, if the Roman Rite of the twenty-first century fails to intersect with the lives of those gathered for worship – if they fail to recognize themselves within the Rite – then the future of Roman Catholic worship is very bleak indeed. The choice is ours.

The future of liturgy, then, is the future of the Church. As it has done in the past, the language of prayer will continue to articulate what the Church believes and what its mission stands for as we move toward the future. May our own commitment to the worship of God in Christ's Church be strengthened. And, as instruments in the service of God, may we dedicate ourselves ever more faithfully to the liturgy of God's world in the service of those most in need, as Christ would have us do.

Notes

1   Marini Interview with John L. Allen, Jr., Archbishop's House, Westminster, London, 15 December 2007, 6.

2   Francis J. Maloney, S.D.B., *A Body Broken for a Broken People: Eucharist in the New Testament* (Peabody, MA: Hendrickson Publishers, 1990, 1997), 155–159.